Dictionary Two

J. Neale

Collins Educational
An imprint of HarperCollins*Publishers*

Aa
Bb
Cc
Dd
Ee
Ff
Gg
Hh
Ii
Jj
Kk
Ll
Mm
Nn
Oo
Pp
Qq
Rr
Ss
Tt
Uu
Vv
Ww
Xx
Yy
Zz

abacus

aborigine

accordion

acorn

adder

Aa

abacus rows of beads used for counting

abandon to leave someone or something, and never return

abbey
1 a church
2 a place where monks or nuns may live

abbreviation a shortened form of a word
(B.B.C. is the abbreviation for British Broadcasting Corporation.)

aborigine the original people of a country especially Australia

about
1 close to
(It was **about** a metre away.)
2 to do with
(I have a book **about** computers.)

above
1 higher than
2 overhead

absent not here; away

accept to take something that is offered

accident something that happens suddenly and may be harmful

accordion a musical instrument, with keys, bellows and buttons

accurate free from mistakes; exactly right

ache a pain, as in headache, toothache, or earache

acorn the nut-like fruit of the oak tree

acrobat someone who does daring leaps and jumps, often on a trapeze

across
1 to the other side of
(He swam **across** the river.)
2 on the other side
(He was safely **across.**)

act
1 something we do
2 a law made by parliament
3 to take part in a play

active lively; busy

actor (actress) someone who performs in films, on TV, or on the stage

add
1 to find the total of two or more numbers
2 to put one thing to another

adder a small, poisonous snake

address
1 the place where a person lives or works
2 where a letter or package is to go

admiral a high-ranking officer in the navy

advertise

admire to think highly of something or someone

admit 1 to allow to enter
(This ticket will **admit** two people.)
2 to agree that something has happened
(She had to **admit** that she was wrong.)

adore to love very much

adult a grown-up person

advance to move forward

adventure an exciting happening

advertise to make well known

advice helpful suggestions

aerial a wire frame to pick up or send out radio or television signals

aeroplane a flying machine

afford to spare money or time for something

afraid full of fear; frightened

after 1 behind
(She came into the room **after** her brother.)
2 at a later time
(We went swimming **after** breakfast.)

afternoon the time between noon and evening

again once more

against 1 touching; next to
(The boy leaned **against** the fence.)
2 opposite to
(The sailors fought **against** the pirates.)

age how many years a person has lived or a thing has lasted

ago before this time

agree to think in the same way as someone else

agriculture farming

ahead in front of

aid help; assistance

aim 1 to plan to do something
2 to point at a target

air 1 what we breathe
2 to warm clothes so they are dry

aircraft any flying machine

air hostess a woman who looks after people in an aircraft

airliner an aircraft which carries passengers

air hostess

airliner

album

alligator

ambulance

amphibian

airport a place where aircraft land and take off

alarm
1 the feeling of fear
2 a warning signal of danger

album a book to hold a collection of things like stamps or photographs

alike nearly the same

alive living

all everyone; everything

alligator a large reptile, found in the rivers of some warm countries

allow to let someone do something

almost nearly

alone without anyone else

along from one end to the other
(The man walked **along** the main street.)

aloud able to be heard

alphabet the letters of a language; A.B.C. etc

already before this time; by now

also as well; too

altar the holy table in a church

alter to change

although even though; in spite of
(**Although** it was true, they did not believe it.)

altogether counting everyone or everything
(**Altogether** there were seven people in the room.)

aluminium a light metal

always forever; every time

amaze to surprise very much

ambulance a van for carrying injured or ill people to hospital

ammunition bullets and shells for guns

among/amongst in the middle of; mixed with

amount
1 a sum of money
2 a number or quantity of several things together

amphibian an animal that can live on both land and in the water

amuse to make someone laugh or smile

anchor a heavy metal hook, dropped to the bottom of the water to stop a ship moving

ancient very old; belonging to past ages

and as well as

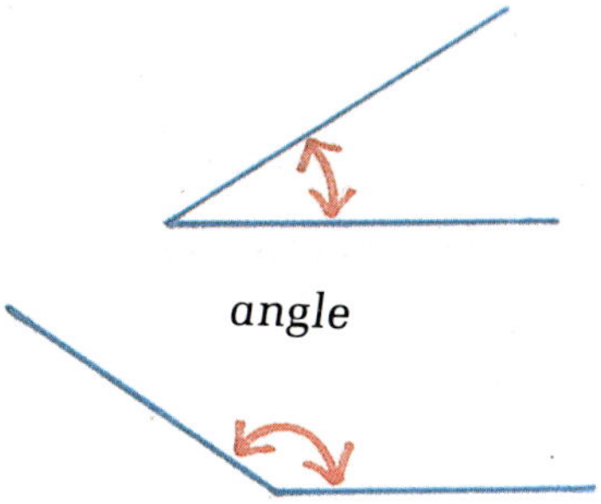

angle

antelope

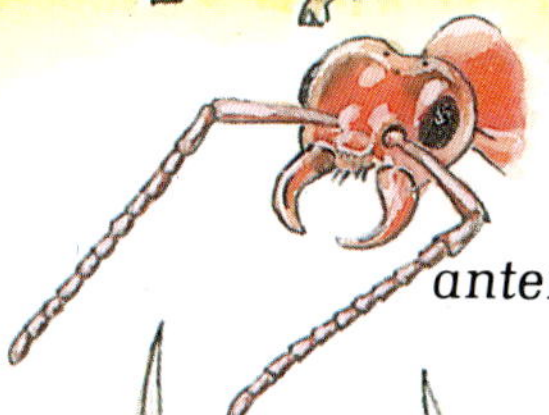

antenna

antlers

aquarium

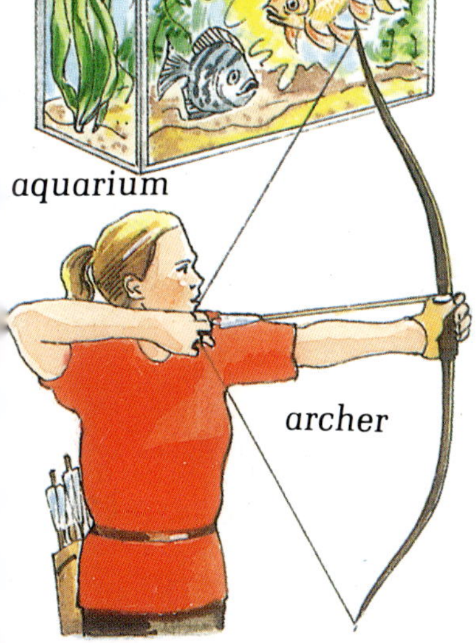

archer

angel	a messenger of God
angle	a corner where two lines meet
angler	someone who fishes with rod and line
angry	bad-tempered; in a rage
animal	any living thing that is not a plant
ankle	the joint between the foot and leg
announce	to let people know something
annoy	to trouble someone; to make someone angry
annual	happening once each year
anorak	a short coat with a hood
another	*1* one more *2* different
answer	what we say when we are asked a question
ant	a small, busy insect
antarctic	at or near the South Pole
antelope	a swift animal like a deer
antenna	one of two feelers on the head of a crab, lobster or insect
antique	something made long ago, often a piece of furniture
antlers	the horns of deer, moose etc
any	one of several
anybody	any person
anywhere	in any place
apart	separate; alone
ape	a kind of monkey with no tail
apologize	to say you are sorry for something
appear	to come into sight
appetite	the feeling of wanting food
applause	clapping hands, cheering
apple	a fruit that is good to eat
approach	to come near to
apricot	a soft fruit which looks like a small peach
apron	a piece of clothing worn to keep clothes clean when working
aquarium	a tank for fish
arch	a curved part of a building
archer	a person who shoots arrows with a bow

architect	someone who plans and designs buildings
arctic	at or near the North Pole
area	the size of a flat space or surface
argue	to disagree with someone
arise	to get up
arithmetic	working with numbers
arm	the part of the body between the shoulder and the hand
armchair	a chair with an arm on each side of the seat
armour	metal clothing worn by soldiers in old times
army	a great number of soldiers
around	on all sides, in a circle
arrange	*1* to set in order *2* to make plans
arrest	to take and keep someone prisoner
arrive	to reach a place after a journey
arrow	a pointed stick with feathers at one end, shot from a bow
artificial	not real or natural
artist	a person skilled at painting, drawing or sculpture
ash	*1* a kind of tree *2* the dust left after a fire
ashamed	feeling unhappy and sorry about something you have done
ask	to question someone
asleep	not awake
ass	a donkey; looks like a small horse with long ears
assembly	the time when people come together
assist	to help
astonish	to surprise greatly
astronaut	a traveller in space
astronomy	the study of the stars, planets, sun, moon etc
athlete	a person who is active in sports
atlas	a book of maps
atmosphere	the air round the earth
attach	to join together
attack	to begin to fight; to set upon
attempt	to try to do something

auction

avalanche

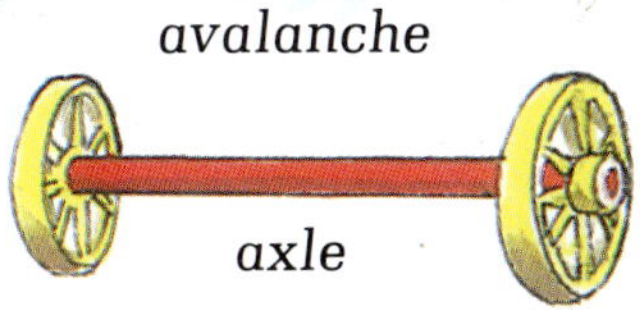
axle

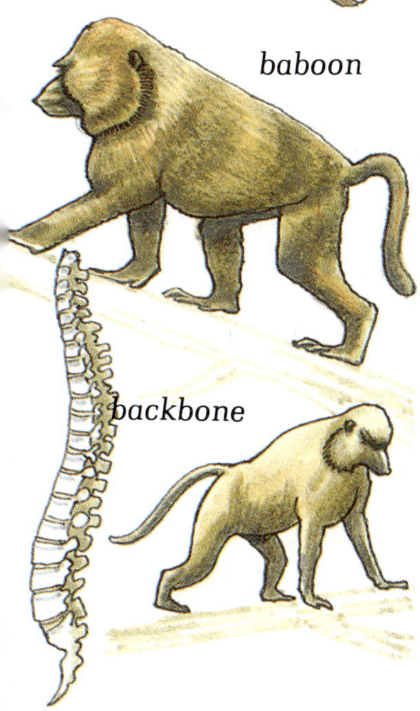
baboon

backbone

attic — a room just under the roof of a house

attract — to pull to itself
(A magnet will **attract** metal nails.)

auction — a sale where each thing is sold to the person who will give the most money for it

audience — people who listen or watch

aunt — a sister of your father or mother; an uncle's wife

author — a writer of books

autograph — a person's name written by themselves

automatic — working by itself

autumn — the season between summer and winter

avalanche — a heavy fall of snow and rocks down a mountain side

avenue — a road or street, often one lined with trees

average — usual; ordinary
(The **average** person likes TV.)

avoid — to keep clear of; to keep away from

awake — not asleep

away — not here

awful — very bad; terrible

awkward —
1 not easy to handle
2 clumsy

axe — a sharp tool for cutting wood

axle — the pole or rod on which a wheel turns

Bb

baboon — a kind of large African monkey

baby — a very young child

babysitter — a person who looks after young children

bachelor — a man who is not married

back —
1 the part of anything which is behind
2 in return
(Jean gave the ball **back** to the boy.)

backbone — the spine; a line of small bones down the back of your body

backwards — facing the wrong way

bacon — meat from a pig, salted and sometimes smoked

bad —
1 not good
2 rotten

badge a special sign worn on clothes showing that you belong to a certain group, or have a special job

badger a grey, hairy animal which digs holes in the ground for its home

badminton a game like tennis, played on a court, with a racket and shuttlecock

bag a container in which things are carried

baggage cases and bags that people take when they travel

bagpipes a musical instrument with a bag and pipes

bait something put in a trap or on a hook to catch animals or fish

bake to cook in an oven

baker someone whose job is to bake bread, pies and cakes

balance
1 to keep steady
2 weighing scales

bald having no hair on the head

bale a bundle of hay or straw

ball something round, like a sphere

ballerina a female ballet dancer

ballet a story or play told in the form of graceful dancing

balloon
1 a toy; a coloured rubber bag that is filled with air
2 a kind of aircraft; a large bag filled with hot air that makes it float in the sky

ball-point a pen which has a tiny ball at the end, for writing with

bamboo a very tall grass with stiff hollow stems used as canes in gardens

banana a long, curved fruit with a thick, yellow skin

band
1 a group of musicians playing together
2 a narrow strip used for holding things together such as an elastic band
3 a group of people

bandage a piece of cloth used to cover and tie up a wound

bang a very loud noise

banister the handrail of a staircase

banjo a musical instrument played by plucking the four or five strings

bank
1 the side of a river
2 a building where money is kept safe
3 a heap of earth or snow
4 to turn an aeroplane

banner

barley

barometer

baseball

bat 1

bat 2

beagle

banner a flag

banquet a large feast or dinner party

bar
1 a rod, often of metal
2 a counter where food and drink are sold

barbecue an outdoor meal

barber a person who cuts hair

bare not covered; with nothing on

bargain something that is bought cheaply and is good value for money

barge a flat-bottomed boat used on rivers and canals

bark
1 the cry of a dog
2 the outside cover of a tree trunk or branch

barley a grain, grown like wheat, that is used for food

barn a farm building used for storing crops

barometer an instrument that measures air pressure, and shows changes in the weather

barrel
1 a round, wooden container
2 the tube of a gun

barrow a small cart, usually with one wheel, pushed by hand

base the bottom part; the lowest part

baseball a game played with bat and ball on a field with four bases

basin a dish or bowl

basket a kind of bag made from cane or straw

basketball a game played with a large ball on a court with two nets

bat
1 an animal like a mouse with wings which flies at night
2 a piece of wood used to hit a ball in games such as cricket and baseball

bath a large container in which we wash our bodies

bathe to wash, swim or play in water

bathroom a room where we wash, bath and shower

battery a container for storing electricity

battle a fight between people, or ships or aeroplanes

bawl to shout loudly

bay a big curve of an ocean or a lake into the land

beach the sand or pebbles at the edge of the sea or a lake

beads small pieces of stone, glass or wood which are threaded on a string to make a necklace

beagle a small hound dog

beak

beaver

bee

beetle

beige

beak the mouth of a bird

beaker a tall cup sometimes without a handle

beam a ray of light

bean a seed from a pod, eaten as a vegetable

bear a very large, furry animal

beard hair growing on a man's face

beast
1 an animal
2 an unkind person

beat
1 to keep on hitting
2 to win in a game
3 to mix things by quickly stirring

beautiful lovely; very pretty

beaver a soft, furry animal that lives in water as well as on land

because for this reason

bed
1 a piece of furniture used for sleeping on
2 the bottom of the sea or a river
3 an area of soil in which plants are grown

bedroom a room where we sleep

bee a flying insect that makes honey and wax

beech a large tree which has dark green leaves

beef meat from cattle

beehive a hive or house for bees

beer a strong drink made from malt and hops

beetle an insect with a hard skin to protect its four wings

beetroot a dark-red, root vegetable

before
1 in front of
2 earlier than
3 in time past

beg to ask for food, money and clothes

begin to start to do something

behave to show good or bad manners in front of others

behind at the back of

beige a light brown colour

believe to think that something is true

bell a hollow metal object that gives a ringing sound when struck

bellow to roar, to shout in an angry way

belong
1 to be owned by someone
2 to be a part of
(The girls **belong** to the Girl Guides.)

Bb

bill 1

bill 2

binoculars

bishop 1

bishop 2

bison

below underneath; lower than

belt a narrow piece of material worn round the waist

bench
1 a long, wooden seat
2 a work table

bend
1 a curve
2 to make something into a curved shape
3 to lean over

beneath under, in a lower place

berry a small, juicy fruit such as raspberry

beside by the side of; close to

besides also; as well

best none better

between
1 in the middle of two things
2 one or the other
(Choose **between** the two books.)

beware be on your guard against; to watch out for

beyond on the far side

Bible the holy book of Christians

bicycle a two-wheeled riding machine

big large; tall

bike a short name for bicycle

bill
1 a bird's beak
2 a list showing how much money is owed

billion a very large number, a thousand million (1 000 000 000)

bin a container

bind to tie or fasten together with string, thread or rope

bingo a game of lucky numbers

binoculars two very small telescopes fastened side by side

birch a tree with a smooth bark which peels off like paper

bird a feathered animal that lays eggs and has wings

birth being born

birthday the day of the year when a person is born

biscuit a crisp, small cake

bishop
1 a clergyman in charge of a large area
2 a piece in the game of chess

bison a kind of buffalo that lives in North America

bit
1 a small piece of something
2 a tool for making holes
3 the metal part of a horse's bridle, held in its mouth

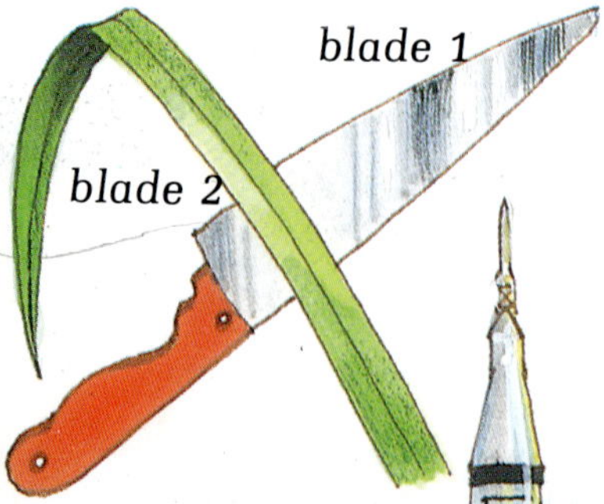

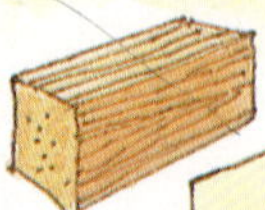

bite	to cut something with the teeth
bitter	having a sharp, sour taste
black	the darkest colour
blackberry	a small, juicy fruit usually growing wild
blackbird	a songbird often seen and heard in gardens
blackboard	a large board for writing or drawing on with chalk
blackcurrant	a small, black fruit that grows on a garden bush
blacksmith	a person who uses tools to make metal things
blade	*1* the sharp part of a knife or tool *2* one leaf of grass
blame	to find fault with someone
blank	not written on; an empty space
blanket	a warm bed-covering
blast	an explosion; a loud sound
blast-off	the moment rockets or missiles leave the ground
blaze	to burn brightly
blazer	a kind of jacket
bleat	the noise made by sheep and lambs
bleed	to lose blood
blind	*1* unable to see *2* a covering for a window
blink	to open and close the eyes quickly
blister	a bubbly swelling on the skin
blizzard	a heavy snowstorm with strong winds
block	*1* a large piece of wood, stone or metal *2* a row of buildings such as a **block** of flats *3* to be in the way of something
blond/blonde	having fair hair and a light skin
blood	the red liquid pumped around your body by your heart
bloodhound	a large dog with a keen sense of smell
blossom	flowers of plants and trees
blot	a dirty mark or spot; an ink stain
blouse	a light garment worn above the waist
blow	*1* a hard knock *2* to send out air from the mouth *3* when air moves fast
blue	the colour of a clear, cloudless sky
bluebell	a wild plant with flowers shaped like bells

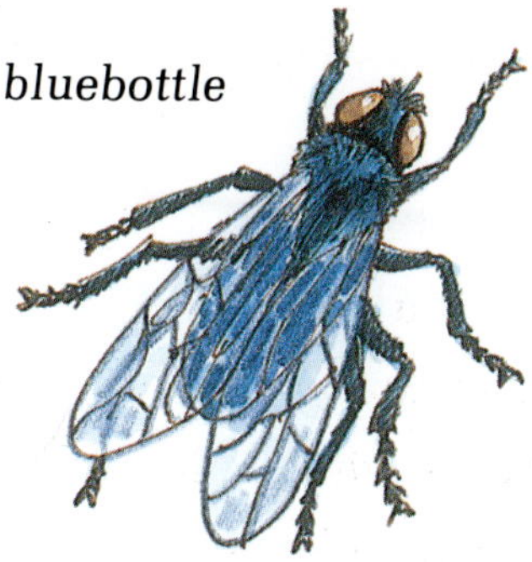

bluebottle

boar

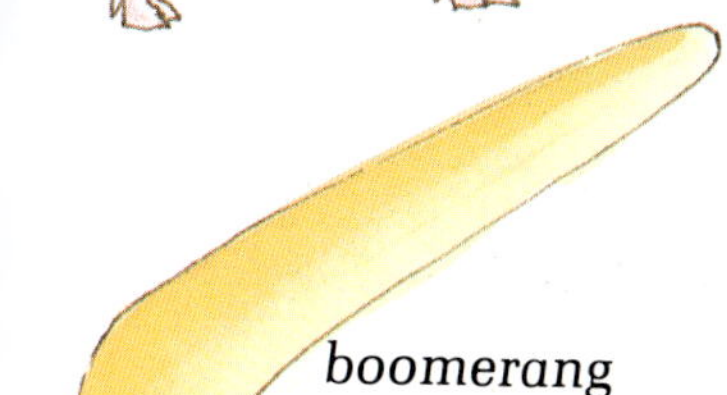

boomerang

boot 1

boot 2

bluebottle a large, buzzing fly with a bluish body

blunt not sharp

blush to go red in the face because you are shy, excited or ashamed

boar a male pig

board
1 a long, flat piece of wood
2 to enter a ship, train or aircraft

boast to praise yourself or to say how good something is that you own

boat
1 a small open ship such as a rowing **boat**
2 a small ship such as a coaster

bob to move up and down

body
1 all the parts of any person or animal
2 a group of people

boil
1 a painful swelling on the skin
2 when a liquid is heated until it bubbles
3 to cook something in boiling water

bolt
1 a sliding bar used to fasten a gate or door
2 to make a sudden dash
3 a metal pin on which a nut can be threaded

bomb a weapon that explodes

bone one of the hard white pieces that make up a skeleton

bonfire a large fire lit outside for pleasure

bonnet
1 a kind of hat
2 the lid of a car's engine

book sheets of paper fastened together for reading or writing in

bookcase a piece of furniture with shelves for books

boomerang an Australian wooden weapon shaped to turn in the air and come back to the thrower

boot
1 a shoe that comes above the ankle
2 the luggage space in a car

border
1 an edge
2 the line on a map where two countries meet

bore
1 to make a hole
2 to make someone tired because you are uninteresting

born brought into life

borrow to take something that has to be given back

boss someone in charge

both the one and the other; the two

bother to cause trouble; to annoy

bough

boxer 1

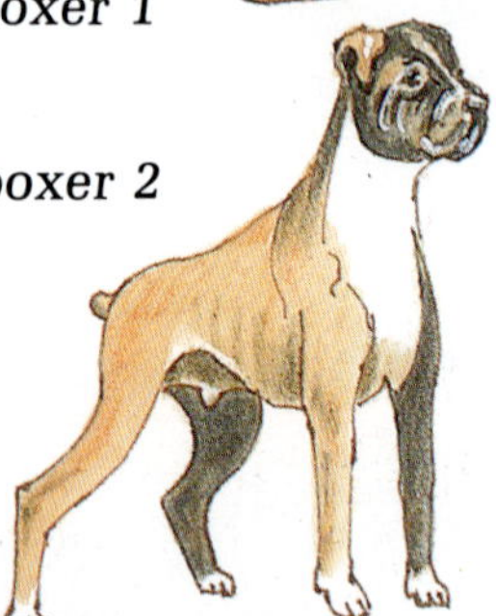

boxer 2

bramble

brand 1

brand 2

bottle		a container for liquids, usually made of glass or plastic
bough		a branch of a tree
boulder		a very large rock or stone
bounce		to throw something (such as a ball) so that it will come back
bouquet		a bunch of flowers
boutique		a small shop selling modern clothes
bow (like low)	*1*	a weapon for shooting arrows
	2	a ribbon tied in loops
bow (like cow)	*1*	the front part of a ship
	2	to bend forward from the waist, to show respect
bowl	*1*	a dish or basin, usually round
	2	to send the ball to a batsman
bowls		a game in which big balls are rolled as near as possible to a small ball called the jack
box	*1*	a container with straight sides
	2	to fight with gloves
boxer	*1*	a man who fights with his fists
	2	a tall, brown dog
boy		a male child
bracelet		a piece of jewellery worn on the wrist
brag		to boast; to show off
brain		the matter in our heads with which we think
brake		the part of a vehicle or machine which makes it slow down or stop
bramble		a blackberry bush
branch		a part of the tree growing out from the trunk
brand	*1*	a certain make of a product
	2	the mark on sheep and cattle to show the owner
brass		a yellow metal made by mixing copper and zinc
brave		not afraid
bray		the sound a donkey makes
bread		a food made by baking a mixture of flour, yeast and water
break	*1*	to smash; to pull apart
	2	a short rest
breakfast		the first meal of the day
breast		the chest
breath		the air that is taken into and let out of the lungs
breathe		to take air into the body and let it out again

Bb

bricklayer

bridegroom *bride* *bridesmaid*

broccoli *Brussels sprouts*

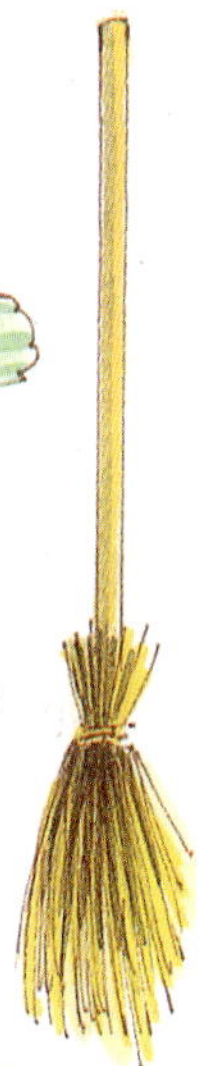

uffalo

breeze	a gentle wind
brewery	where beer is made
brick	a block of baked clay for building
bricklayer	a person who builds with bricks
bride	a woman on her wedding day
bridegroom	a man on his wedding day
bridesmaid	a girl or woman who helps a bride at a wedding
bridge	something built to cross a river, road or railway
brief	short; not taking long
bright	*1* giving out light; shining *2* clever
brilliant	shining brightly
brim	the edge of a cup or bowl
bring	to fetch or carry something
brittle	easily broken or snapped
broad	very wide
broadcast	to send out a programme on radio or television
broccoli	a dark green vegetable
bronze	a metal made by melting copper and tin together
brooch	a piece of jewellery fastened to clothing by a pin
brood	*1* to worry over something in a quiet, moody way *2* a number of young birds all hatched together
brook	a small stream
broom	a long-handled brush for sweeping
brother	a boy who has the same parents as you do
brow	the forehead
brown	a dark colour, like that of coffee or chocolate
brush	a tool used for cleaning, scrubbing, sweeping or painting
Brussels sprouts	very small, green, cabbage-like vegetables
bubble	a very thin ball of liquid filled with air
bucket	a container with a handle, for carrying water
buckle	a fastening on a belt or shoe
bud	a flower or leaf before it opens
budgerigar	a small bird with colourful markings often kept as a pet
buffalo	a large, wild ox
bugle	a small trumpet

bulb 1

bulb 2

bulldog

bulldozer

buoy

burrow

by-pass

build to put together; to make something

building something that is built such as a house, school, shop or office block

bulb
1 the part of an electric lamp that gives light
2 the round root, shaped like an onion, of some plants

bulge to swell out or curve outwards

bull the male of cattle

bulldog a heavy dog with a flattened face

bulldozer a powerful tractor that moves soil and rocks

bullet a piece of metal fired from a rifle or revolver

bully someone who frightens or hurts a weaker person

bump
1 to knock against something
2 a swelling on the body

bun a small, soft, round cake

bunch a group of things growing or fastened together

bundle a collection of things tied together

bungalow a house with all its rooms on the ground floor

bunk a bed in a ship's cabin

buoy a marker floating in the sea used to warn ships of danger

burglar someone who breaks in to steal

burn
1 to be on fire
2 a sore place on the skin caused by heat

burrow a hole in the ground dug and lived in by animals

burst to break open suddenly; to blow into pieces

bury to put under the ground

bus a motor vehicle for carrying people to and from places

bush a shrub; a small tree with many branches

bus stop where a bus picks up and drops passengers

busy having much to do

butcher a person who cuts up and sells meat

butter a yellow food made from cream

buttercup a small, wild flower with yellow petals

butterfly a flying insect with four brightly coloured wings

button a fastening for clothes

buy to obtain something by giving money

buzz the humming sound as made by a flying bee

bypass a road going around a busy town to avoid the traffic

cab 1

cab 2

cactus

camel

canal

canyon

Cc

cab
1 a car that you can hire with a driver; a taxi
2 the part in a lorry, bus or train where the driver sits

cabbage
a large, round, green vegetable

cabin
1 a small room in a ship
2 a wooden hut

cactus
a very prickly plant that grows in the desert

café
a place where snacks and meals are sold

cage
a box or room with bars for keeping birds or other animals

cake
a sweet made from flour and baked in an oven

calculator
a machine that can rapidly add, subtract, multiply, divide etc

calendar
a list of days, weeks and months of the year

calf
1 a young cow, bull, elephant or whale
2 the back of your leg below the knee

call
1 to shout
2 to visit someone's house
3 to telephone someone
4 to name someone
(We **call** her Susan.)

calm
quiet and still; not windy

camel
a desert animal with one or two humps on its back

camera
a machine which takes photographs

camp
1 a place where a group of tents are set up
2 to stay and sleep out of doors

can
1 a metal container
2 to be allowed to
(You **can** go to the football match.)
3 to be able to
(I **can** skate on ice.)

canal
a waterway dug across land

canary
a yellow songbird, often kept as a pet

cancel
to stop something that has been arranged

candle
a stick of wax with a wick in it, burned to give light

cannon
a large, old-fashioned gun

canoe
a small, narrow boat moved by paddles

canyon
a steep valley

cap
1 a soft hat with a peak
2 a lid for a container

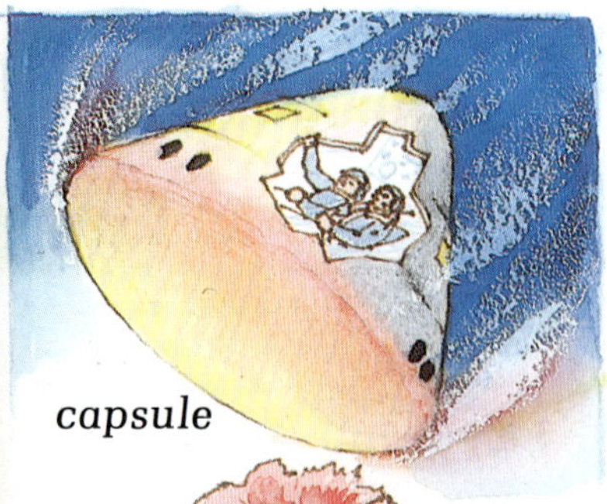
capsule

carnation

carport

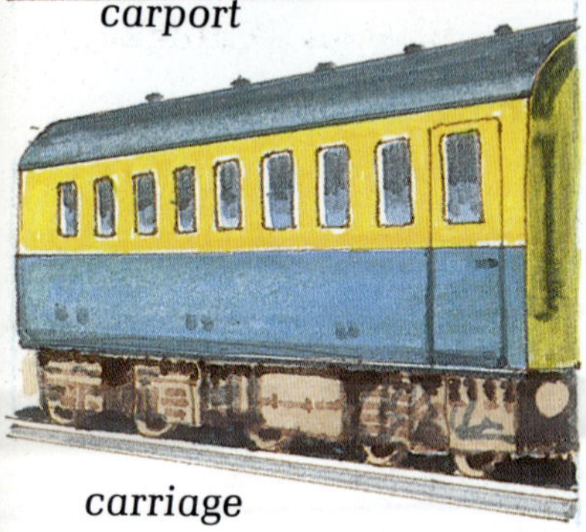
carriage

carrot

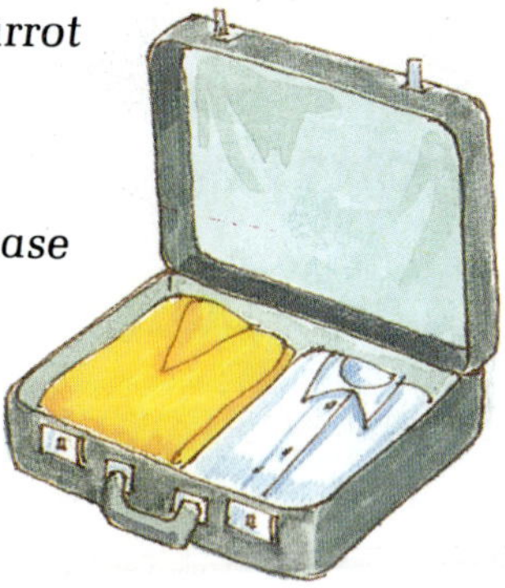
case

capital
1 the chief city of a country
(Canberra is the **capital** of Australia.)
2 a large letter such as A, E, or M

capsize to overturn a boat in the water

capsule the part of a spaceship occupied by the astronauts

captain
1 the person in charge of a ship
2 an officer in the army
3 the leader of a sports team

capture to take prisoner; to catch

car a motor vehicle to carry people

caravan a small house on wheels often pulled by a car

card thick paper

cardboard stiff board made from paper

cardigan a short, knitted jacket

care
1 to look after
2 to feel interested or to mind
3 to be cautious
(Take **care** when you cross the road.)

careful taking care

careless not taking care

caretaker someone who looks after a building

cargo goods carried on a ship or an aircraft

carnation a plant with sweet-smelling flowers

carnival a parade, usually in fancy dress

carol a song usually sung at Christmas

carpenter someone who makes things from wood

carpet a thick, soft floor covering

carport a shelter for a car, often built against the side of a house

carriage a vehicle for carrying passengers; a railway **carriage**

carrot a vegetable with a long, orange root

carry to take something from one place to another

cart a vehicle used for carrying goods

carton a box made of cardboard for holding goods

cartoon
1 a drawing that makes fun of something
2 a film, made from lots of drawings

carve to cut wood or stone into a shape

case a box with a lid, it is used to carry things

cash money in coins and notes

cast the actors performing in a play or a film

catamaran

cello

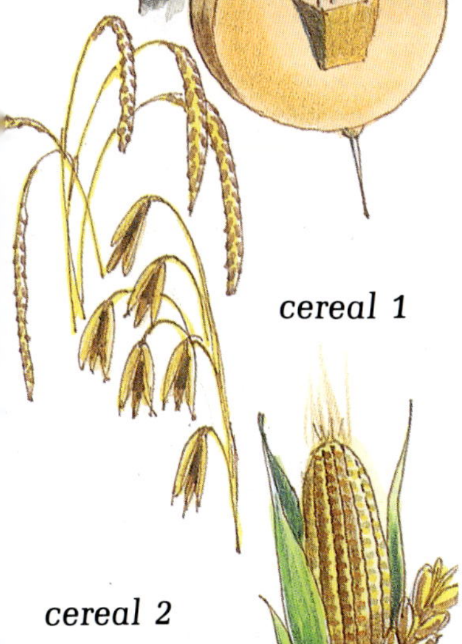
cereal 1

cereal 2

castle an old building with thick stone walls and towers, to be defended against attack

cat a small, furry animal kept as a pet

catalogue a list of things to sell

catamaran a boat with two narrow hulls

catch
1 to take hold of something moving
2 a fastener for a door

caterpillar the grub which will turn into a moth or a butterfly

cathedral the main church of a large district

catkin the fluffy flower of the willow and hazel trees

cattle cows, bulls and calves

cauliflower a vegetable with a white flower head

cave/cavern a hole in rocks or in the earth

cease to stop doing something

cedar an evergreen tree with spreading branches

ceiling the inside top surface of a room

celery a vegetable with white stems

cell a small room in a prison

cellar an underground storeroom

cello a musical instrument with strings, larger than a violin

cement a grey powder used in making concrete

cemetery a burial ground for the dead

cent a coin used in many countries; a hundredth part of a dollar

centigrade a scale for measuring temperature; also called celsius

centimetre a measure of length

centre the middle of something

century a hundred years

cereal
1 any food grain such as rice, oats, wheat and corn
2 a breakfast food made from any of these grains

ceremony a special celebration, sometimes happy and sometimes sad

certain
1 sure
(Are you **certain** you can go?)
2 some, but not all
(I am looking for a **certain** stamp.)

certificate a piece of paper proving that something is true

chain metal rings joined together

chair a seat with a back, for one person

Cc

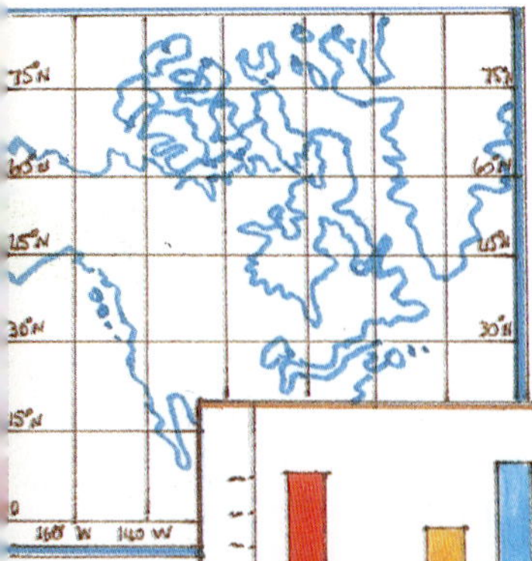
chart 1

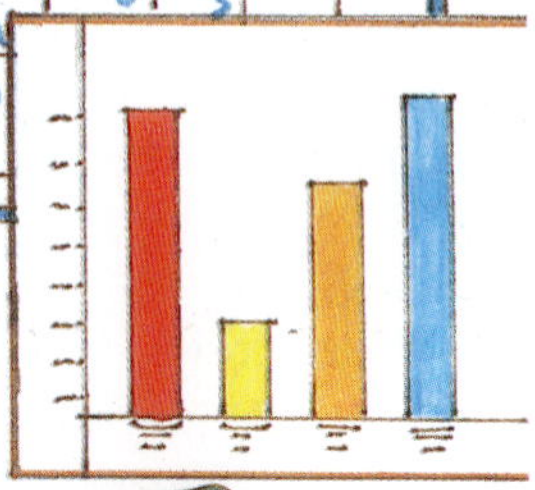
chart 2

chauffeur

cheetah

chestnut

chalk		a soft white rock used for writing on a blackboard
champion		someone who has beaten all the others; the best
chance	1	a lucky or unexpected happening
	2	a risk
change	1	to make something different
	2	money given back when too much is given for payment
channel	1	a narrow stretch of water
	2	a radio or television wavelength
chapel		a place of worship
chapter		a part of a book
charge	1	to ask a price for something
	2	to rush at
charm	1	a pleasant manner
	2	an object thought to bring good luck
chart	1	a map used by sailors
	2	a drawing to show certain facts
chase		to run after
chat		to talk in a friendly way
chauffeur		a person paid to drive someone in a car
cheap		not costing much
check	1	to make sure something is right
	2	a pattern with squares on it
	3	to slow down or stop
cheek	1	the soft side of your face below each eye
	2	rudeness
cheerful		happy and pleasant
cheese		a food made from milk
cheetah		a fast, wild animal of the cat family
chef		the head cook in a restaurant or hotel
chemist		a person who sells all kinds of medicines
cherry		a small, round, red fruit with a stone inside
chess		a game played with special pieces on a board of 64 squares
chest	1	the upper, front part of your body
	2	a strong box with a lid
chestnut		a large tree that bears nuts
chew		to crush and grind food with your teeth
chewing gum		a sweet for chewing
chicken		a young bird

chimpanzee

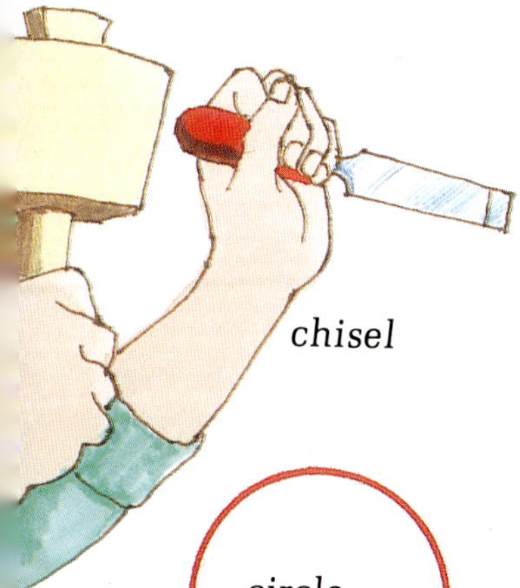

chisel

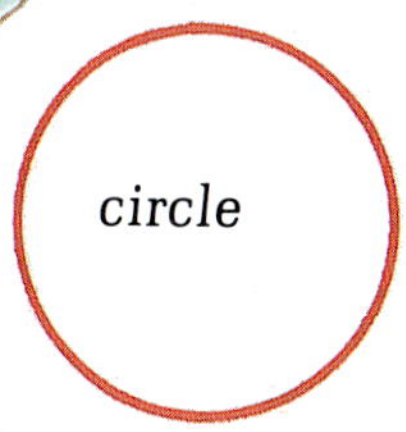

circle

claw

chickenpox	a catching disease; marked by a fever and spots
chief	the most important
child	a young boy or girl
chilly	cold
chime	the sound made by bells
chimney	the part of a building that takes away smoke and fumes
chimpanzee	a kind of African ape
chin	the part of the face below the mouth
china	fine cups, saucers and plates made from special white clay
chips	*1* pieces of fried potato *2* small pieces of wood or stones
chirp	the noise made by some birds
chisel	a cutting tool
chocolate	a sweet made from cocoa
choir	a group of people singing together
choke	to be unable to breathe properly
choose	to pick out
chop	*1* to cut with an axe *2* a slice of meat with its bone
Christian	a person who believes in Jesus Christ
Christmas	the day celebrating the birth of Jesus
chuckle	a quiet laugh
chunk	a thick piece
church	a building where people pray to God
cinema	a place where films are shown
circle	a perfect round shape; a ring
circus	a show given by clowns, acrobats and animals in a ring
city	a very large town
clang	the deep ringing sound of a large bell
clap	*1* to hit the palms of your hands together *2* the sound make by thunder
clasp	to grip firmly
class	a group of children who are taught together
classroom	a room in a school where children learn
claw	the hard nail of a bird and some other animals
clay	stiff, sticky earth used to make bricks and pottery

cliff

clip 1

clip 2

coach 1

coach 2

coach 3

clean		not dirty; washed
clear	*1*	with nothing in the way
	2	easy to see or understand
clerk		someone who works in an office
clever		quick at learning
cliff		high, steep land often overlooking the sea
climate		the kind of weather a place usually has
climb		to go up, often using hands and feet
cling		to hold fast to
clinic		a place where doctors and nurses give help or treatment
clip	*1*	a fastener
	2	to cut with scissors or shears
cloak		a coat without sleeves
cloakroom		a place to leave outdoor clothes
clock		an instrument for telling the time
close (like toes)	*1*	to shut
	2	to come to an end
close (like dose)		very near
clothes		things we wear
cloud		a white or grey mass of tiny drops of water, floating in the sky
clover		a small, wild plant
clown		the funny man of a circus
club	*1*	a heavy stick
	2	a group of people who meet to enjoy some interest together
	3	a long stick with a heavy head for hitting a golf ball
cluck		to make a noise like a hen
clump		a number of flowers or trees growing together
clumsy		awkward in the way we move
clutch		to grab; to hang onto
coach	*1*	a bus
	2	a railway carriage
	3	an instructor, often in sports
coal		a kind of black rock dug out of the ground and burned to make heat
coarse		not smooth; rough
coast		the seashore; where land and sea meet

Cc

cobra

cockroach

coconut

collie

column 1

column 2

combine harvester

coat	*1* an outer garment with sleeves *2* the hair of an animal
cobbler	someone who repairs footwear
cobra	a poisonous snake
cobweb	a net made by a spider to trap insects
cock	a male bird
cockle	a shellfish
cockpit	the place where a pilot of an aeroplane sits
cockroach	a brown beetle
cocoa	*1* a brown powder made from the beans of the cacao tree *2* a hot chocolate drink
coconut	a large, brown nut growing on palm trees
cod	a large seafish which we can eat
code	*1* a set of rules such as the Highway Code *2* signs or writing used to make a secret message
coffee	a hot drink made from the roasted beans of the coffee plant
coil	a wire or rope wound round and round in a spiral
coin	a piece of metal money
cold	*1* not hot *2* an illness causing you to sneeze and cough
collapse	to fall down suddenly; to break down
collar	the part of your clothing that goes round your neck
collect	to bring together
college	a place where people are taught
collide	to bump hard into something
collie	a large shaggy dog with a long, pointed nose
collision	a violent crash together
colonel	an army officer
colour	a dye; a paint
colt	a young male horse
column	*1* a post or pillar *2* a list of numbers or words one below the other
comb	a piece of plastic or metal with teeth, used for tidying your hair
combine	to join together
combine-harvester	a large, farm machine that cuts and threshes grain
come	to move near

comet

compass

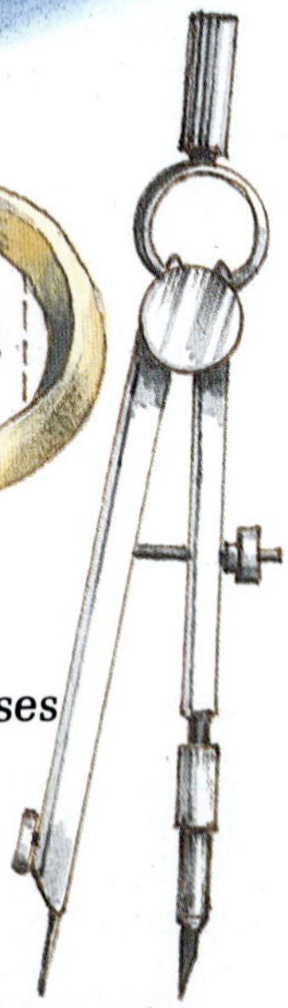
compasses

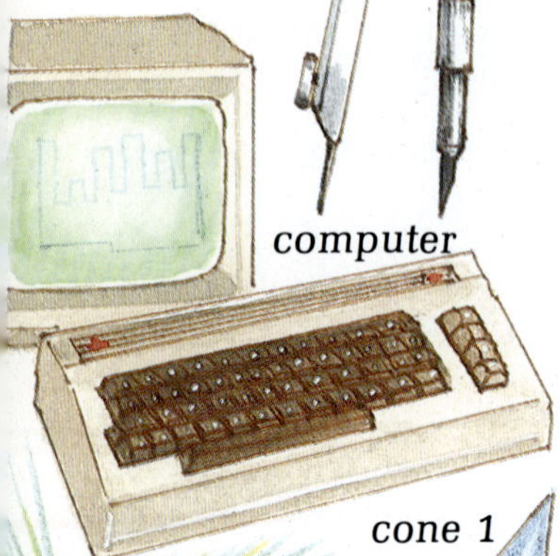
computer

cone 1

cone 2

conker

comedian a performer who makes people laugh

comet a star-like body in the sky, with a long, glowing tail

comfortable contented; at ease

comic
1 funny
2 a picture paper for children

command to order someone to do something

common
1 usual; often seen and found
2 a kind of public park
3 rude in manner

compare to see how people and things differ

compass an instrument showing north, south, east and west

compasses an instrument for drawing circles

complain to grumble; to find fault with something

complete
1 with nothing missing
2 to finish

composer someone who writes music

computer a machine that does calculations quickly and stores information

conceal to hide; to keep secret

concert a performance of music

concrete a mixture of stones, sand, cement and water that sets rock-hard

conduct the way we behave

conductor someone who beats time and directs an orchestra or a choir

cone
1 a shape that is rounded at one end and pointed at the other
2 the woody fruit of an evergreen tree

confess to own up; to admit

confetti tiny bits of coloured paper thrown at the bride and bridegroom after their wedding

confuse to mix up

conjurer someone who does clever tricks that appear magical

conker the shiny, hard, brown nut of the horse-chestnut tree

connect to join one thing to another

conquer to defeat; to overcome in battle

consonant any letter of the alphabet except the vowels a, e, i, o, u

constable a policeman or policewoman

construct to build; to put together

Cc

container		a box, jar, bag etc used to hold something
content		happy with things
contents		the things inside something
contest		a game or race that people try to win
continent		one of the large land masses of the world (Europe, Asia, Africa, North America, South America Australia and Antarctica are the seven **continents.**)
continue		to keep on doing something
control		to have power over; to guide
convent		a house where nuns live and work
cook	*1*	to make food ready by heating it
	2	a person who prepares food
cooker		a gas or electric stove for cooking food
cool		slightly cold
copper		a reddish-brown metal
copse		a small group of trees
copy	*1*	anything made to look like something else
	2	to imitate; to do the same as somebody else
cord		a thick string or thin rope
core		the centre of a thing
cork	*1*	the bark of the cork oak tree
	2	a stopper for a bottle
corn	*1*	the seeds of grain used as food
	2	a sore, hard lump on your foot
corner		a place where two lines, roads or walls etc meet
cornet	*1*	a cone-shaped wafer for ice-cream
	2	a musical instrument like a small trumpet
corpse		a dead body
correct		having no mistakes; true
corridor		a long, narrow passage in a building
cosmonaut		a Russian space traveller
cost		the price of anything
costume	*1*	a style of dress
	2	clothes worn by actors in a play
cosy		warm and snug
cot		a baby's bed, with sides
cottage		a small house, usually in the country
cotton		thread or cloth made from the cotton plant
couch		a long, soft seat like a settee

counter 1

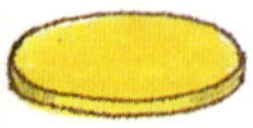
counter 2

court 1

court 2

cowboy

crater

cough the noise made when someone has a cold on the chest

council a group of people chosen to rule something, such as a town **council**

count
1 to add numbers
2 to number in the correct order

countdown the time just before the firing of a missile or rocket

counter
1 a type of table at which customers are served in a shop or bank
2 a small, round marker

country
1 the land outside towns
2 the land where a nation of people lives

couple a pair; two of anything

courage bravery; being able to meet danger

course
1 the direction that something takes when it is moving (The ship's **course** was set for Sydney.)
2 an area for a sport or game — a golf course
3 a part of a meal

court
1 an area where some game is played; a tennis **court**
2 a place where justice is carried out

cousin the child of your aunt or uncle

cover something put on top of another thing, usually to protect or hide it

cow
1 a female of cattle from which we get milk
2 a female whale or elephant

coward someone who runs away from trouble or danger

cowboy a man who looks after cattle in North America

crab a shellfish with eight legs and two pincers

crack
1 a loud, sharp noise
2 a split or thin opening

cracker
1 a thin crisp biscuit
2 a paper toy which bangs when its ends are pulled, used especially at Christmas

cradle a bed for a young baby

crane
1 a machine for lifting heavy weights
2 a long-legged bird

crash
1 a loud noise of breaking
2 to hit against and be smashed

crater the opening of a volcano

crawl to move slowly on hands and knees

crayon a coloured stick of chalk or wax, used for drawing

Cc

cress

cricket 1

cricket 2
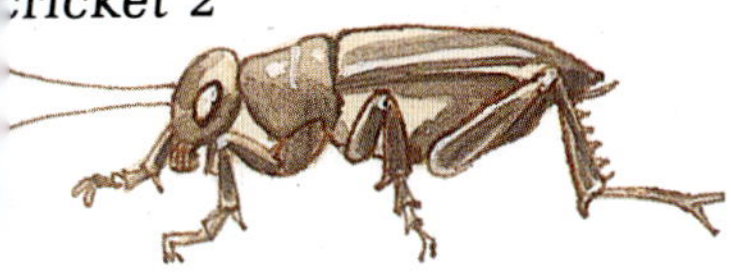

crocodile

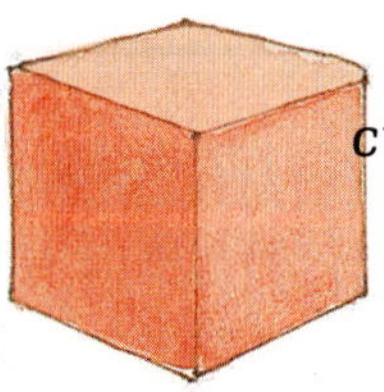
cube

cuckoo

crazy mad; silly

creak a small, squeaking noise

cream the thick liquid found on the top of milk

crease a mark made when cloth or paper is folded

creature any living person or animal

creek
1 a place where a stream flows into the sea
2 a stream

creep to move very slowly and quietly

cress a green plant used in salads

crew the people who work on a ship or an aircraft

cricket
1 a game played with bats, wickets and a ball
2 an insect that looks like a grasshopper

crime a serious breaking of the law

crimson a deep red colour

crisps very thin slices of fried potato

croak the noise a frog makes

crocodile a large reptile with a pointed snout found in the rivers and lakes of some warm countries

crocus a small, spring flower grown from a corm

crooked twisted; not straight

crop plants grown for food

cross
1 angry
2 a mark shaped like + or ×
3 to go from one side to another

crow a big, black bird with a loud, rough call

crowd a great number of people

crown
1 the head-dress of a king or queen
2 the top of anything

cruel very unkind; causing pain

crumb a tiny bit of bread, cake etc

crush to press together very tightly

crust a hard outer covering, such as a pie-crust or the crust of bread

cry
1 to shout out loudly
2 to shed tears

cub a young fox, bear, wolf, lion etc

cube a block with six square faces, or sides, all the same size

cuckoo a bird that lays eggs in other birds' nests

cucumber

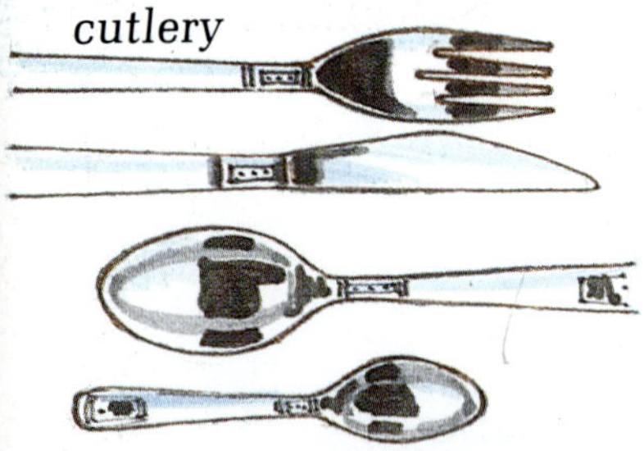
cutlery

cyclone
cygnet

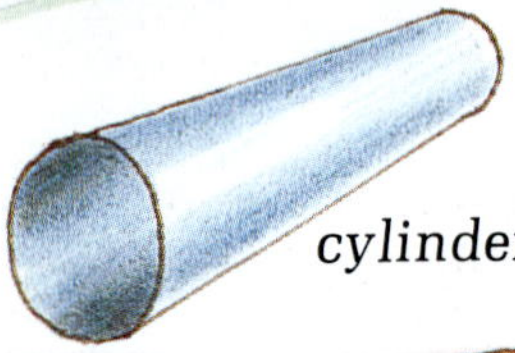
cylinder

dachshund

daffodil

cucumber a long, thin green vegetable used in salads

cuddle to hug someone

cup a small container with a handle, used for drinking

cupboard a set of shelves for storing things, with doors on the front

cure
1 to make a sick person better
2 to preserve food by salting or smoking

curious
1 keen to know about things
2 unusual; strange

currant
1 a small dried grape
2 the fruit of currant bushes

currency the money of a country
(The **currency** of the USA, Australia and New Zealand is the dollar.)

current moving air, water or electricity

curry hot, spicy food

curtain cloth hanging down to cover windows

curve a smooth bend

cushion a soft pillow for a chair or settee

custard a sweet sauce eaten with puddings, pies etc

customer a person who buys things

cut to open or separate with a sharp object such as scissors or a knife

cutlery knives, forks and spoons

cycle
1 a bicycle
2 to ride a bicycle

cyclone a violent storm with winds moving in a spiral towards the centre

cygnet a young swan

cylinder a hollow or solid object that is shaped like a tube

cymbals brass plates used by a drummer to make a clashing sound

Dd

dachshund a small dog with a long body and short legs

dad/daddy father

daddy longlegs a type of flying insect with long legs

daffodil a spring flower that grows from a bulb

dagger a short pointed knife

Dd

dahlia		a brightly-coloured garden flower
daily		every day
dairy		a place where milk is kept and butter and cheese are made
daisy		a very common small flower with a yellow centre and white petals
Dalmatian		a large dog whose white coat is covered with black spots
dam		a wall built to hold back water
damage		to harm; injure
damp		slightly wet
damson		a fruit like a small plum
dance		to move around in time to music
dandelion		a yellow, wild flower
dandruff		small, white pieces of dead skin that collect among the hair
danger		something that can do harm
dangerous		not safe
dangle		to hang or swing loosely
dare		to take a risk
dark		without light
dart	*1*	to move quickly and suddenly
	2	a small arrow for throwing at a board
dash	*1*	to move fast hurriedly
	2	a small line (—)
date	*1*	the day, month and year when something takes place
	2	the fruit of a palm tree
daughter		a girl child
dawdle		to waste time; to go slowly
dawn		daybreak; sunrise
day	*1*	a period of 24 hours
	2	the time between sunrise and sunset
daytime		the time when it is light
dazzle		to blind briefly with bright light
dead		not alive
deaf		not able to hear
dear	*1*	costing a lot of money
	2	loved very much by someone
decade		ten years
decay		to rot away

decorate

deer

deliver

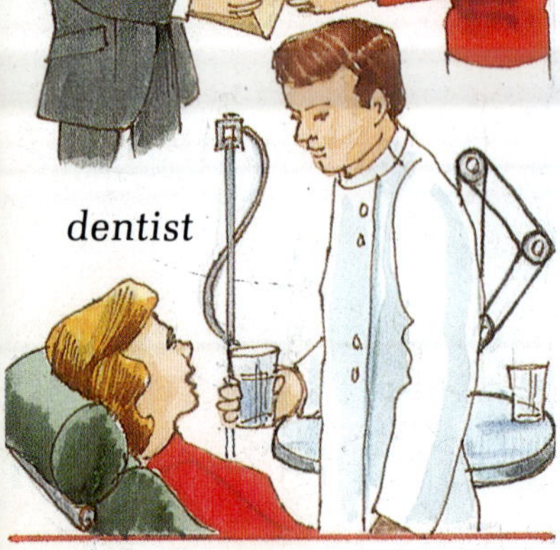
dentist

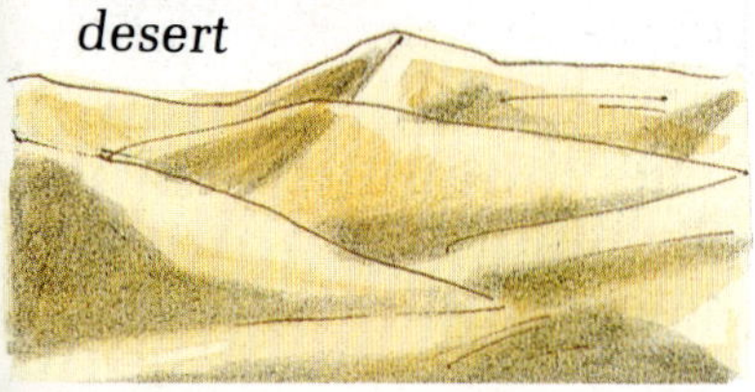
desert

decide	to make up your mind
decimal	having to do with tens or tenths
deck	a floor on a ship, aeroplane or bus
decorate	to make something look pretty
decrease	to grow smaller; to become less
deed	something done; an action
deep	going a long way down
deer	a fast-running, timid animal
defeat	to beat someone in a game or contest
defend	to protect; to guard from attack
delay	to put off doing something for a time
deliberate	done on purpose
delicious	very tasty and good to eat
delightful	very pleasing
deliver	to hand over something to someone
demand	to ask firmly for something
demolish	to pull down or destroy
den	the home of certain wild animals
dentist	a person who looks after your teeth
deny	to say something is not true
deodorant	a substance that hides unpleasant smells
depart	to go away, to leave
depend	to rely on; to trust
deposit	money left in part payment for something
depot	a storehouse, a warehouse
depth	how deep something is
descend	to go down; to come down
describe	to tell or write about something or someone
desert	land where nothing or very little grows
deserve	to earn something by doing well
design	*1* a plan for building or other object *2* a pattern
desk	a table, often with drawers, at which you can write, read etc
destination	the place you are travelling to
destroy	to ruin completely; to wreck
detective	a police officer who tries to solve a crime

Dd

diary

dinosaur

directory

disco

detest to hate very much

dew drops of water that settle on the ground during the night

diagram a drawing to explain something

dial
1 the face of a clock, speedometer, compass etc
2 to make a phone call

diamond a very hard precious stone

diary a book in which you write down what happens each day

dice small cubes with a different number of spots marked on each side

dictionary a book that lists words in alphabetical order, and gives their meanings.

die to stop living

diesel engine an engine that burns fuel oil

diet the food you normally eat

difference the way in which one thing is unlike another

different not the same as

difficult not easy to do; hard to understand

dig to turn soil over with a spade

dim not bright or clear

dinghy a small boat

dining room a room where meals are eaten

dinner the main meal of the day

dinosaur a huge reptile that lived millions of years ago

dip
1 to place into a liquid for a short time
2 to slope down

direct
1 to tell someone the way
2 to order; to tell someone what to do

directory a book containing lists of names

dirty not clean; needing to be washed

disagree to think differently; not to agree

disappear to pass out of sight; to vanish

disappoint to make someone sad by not doing what had been hoped

disaster a great misfortune, accident or tragedy

disc something which is round and flat

disco a discotheque; people dancing to pop records

discover to find out; to see for the very first time

discuss to talk about something with other people

disguise

ditch

diver

dolphin

donkey

dove

disease	an illness; sickness
disguise	to change your appearance in order that people will not know you
dish	*1* a plate or bowl for food *2* a kind of food
dishonest	not able to be trusted
dislike	not to like
disobey	not to do what one is told
distance	the space between two places
district	a part of a town or country
ditch	a long, narrow trench dug in the ground to drain away water
dive	to plunge head first, usually into water
diver	someone who works underwater in a special suit
divide	to share out (**Divide** the sweets among yourselves.)
dizzy	a feeling that things are spinning round and round
dock	a place where ships are loaded and unloaded
doctor	a person trained to look after our health
dodge	to move quickly out of the way
doe	a female rabbit or deer
dog	a four-legged, barking animal often kept as a pet
doll	a toy which looks like a baby or child
dollar	a unit of money used in some countries such as USA, Australia and New Zealand
dolphin	a sea animal like a small whale
donkey	an ass; an animal with long ears and looks like a small horse
door	the entrance into a room or a building
dose	the amount of medicine to be taken at one time
dot	a small spot
double	*1* to make twice as big *2* to fold into two
doubt	not to be sure; feel uncertain
dough	a thick, floury mixture for making bread
doughnut	a small, round piece of fried cake usually with a hole in the centre
dove	a kind of pigeon

dragon

dragonfly

drum 1

drum 2

duck 1

duck 2

down
1 the very soft feathers of a bird
2 at or to a lower place

doze to have a light sleep

dozen a group of twelve

drag to pull something along

dragon a made-up winged monster that breathes fire

dragonfly a large insect that has long legs and two pairs of wings

drain a ditch or pipe that carries away waste water

draught a stream of air

draughts a game played with counters on a board of 64 squares

draw
1 to make a picture using pencil, crayon or chalk
2 neither side having won or lost
(The football match ended in a **draw.**)

drawbridge a bridge that can be raised or lowered

drawer a sliding box in a piece of furniture

drawing-pin a pin with a large, flat head

dream what you seem to see when you are asleep

drench to make wet through

dress
1 a piece of outer clothing worn by girls and women
2 to put on your clothes

drier a machine for drying things

drift to be carried along by currents of air or water

drill a tool used for making holes

drink to swallow some liquid

drip something falling in drops

drive
1 to steer and control a vehicle
2 a wide path leading to a house

drizzle a fall of very light rain

drone
1 a male bee
2 to make a low humming noise

drop
1 to let something fall
2 a tiny spot of liquid

drought a long period without any rain

drown to die under water

drum
1 a musical instrument which is played by beating it with sticks or the hands
2 a large metal container for liquids

dry not wet or even damp

duck
1 a swimming bird with a flat beak and webbed feet
2 to bob down quickly

duet

duffel-coat

dwarf

eagle

easel

eclipse

duet	a piece of music for two players or singers
duffel-coat	a thick coat with a fitted hood
dull	*1* not bright *2* not clever
dumb	not able to speak
during	while something lasts
dusk	the time just before it gets dark in the evening
dust	tiny specks of dry dirt
dustbin	a container to hold rubbish
duster	a cloth for removing dust
dwarf	a very small person
dwell	to live in some place
dye	a liquid or powder used to colour materials

Ee

each	every single one
eager	very keen
eagle	a large, powerful bird that hunts small animals
ear	the part of the body that allows you to hear
early	before the right time
earn	to get payment for working
earrings	decorations for the ears
earth	*1* the world where we live *2* the soil we plant things in
earthquake	sudden strong shaking of the earth
easel	a stand on which to rest a picture
east	the direction of sunrise; the opposite to west
Easter	the time when Christians celebrate the rising of Jesus from the dead
easy	simple; not difficult
eat	to take food through the mouth
ebony	a very hard, black wood
echo	a sound that bounces back when you shout at a wall of a rock or inside a cave.
eclipse	a time when the moon comes between the earth and the the sun and blocks its light
edge	a rim or border

editor — a person in charge of a newspaper, magazine or book

educate — to teach or train people

eel — a snake-like fish

effort — hard work; a good try

egg — a roundish object with a thin shell or skin laid by birds, fish, reptiles etc

either — one or the other of two

elastic — a material that stretches and then goes back to its own length

elbow — the joint in the middle of the arm

elderly — old

election — choosing by vote

electrician — a person who puts in or repairs electrical equipment

electricity — a power used to make light or heat and drive machines

elephant — a huge animal with a trunk, large ears and sometimes tusks

elevator — *1* a vehicle for carrying people or things up and down; a lift
2 a building for storing grain

elf — in stories, a small mischievous fairy

elk — a large deer of North America

elm — a tall, broad-leaved tree

elsewhere — in some other place

emerald — a bright green precious stone

emergency — a sudden happening that requires very prompt action

empty — with nothing inside

emu — a large, flightless, Australian bird

encourage — to help by giving hope

encyclopedia — a big book, or set of books, with facts and information about many different subjects

end — the last part; the finish

enemy — one who is against you and wishes to harm you

energy — the strength to do things

engine — a machine that does work or makes something move

enjoy — to like doing something

enormous — very large; huge

enough — as much or as many as you need

enter — to go into or come into

entertain to amuse and make people happy

entrance a way in; a doorway

envelope a folded cover or wrapper for a letter

equal of the same size or value

equator an imaginary circle around the middle of the world

errand a short journey to collect or deliver something

error a mistake

escalator a moving staircase

escape to get away; to become free

Eskimo one of a race of people living in the cold lands of the north

estate a number of houses built in one place

estimate to guess the size, amount, or value of something

eucalyptus a tall tree, such as the Australian gum tree

eve the night before an important day
(People enjoy parties on New Year's **Eve.**)

even
1 smooth; level
2 equal; no more nor less than
3 able to be divided by two without a remainder

evening the time between the afternoon and night

event some special happening

ever at any time; always

evergreen a plant or tree with green leaves all the year round

everybody all the people

everything each thing; all things

everywhere in every place

evil very wicked; harmful

ewe a female sheep

exactly without mistake; just right

examine to test; to look at carefully

example one thing taken to show what the others are like or should be like

excavate to dig out from the earth

excellent very, very good

except other than; leaving out

exchange to give one thing in return for another

excite to thrill; to stir up strong feeling

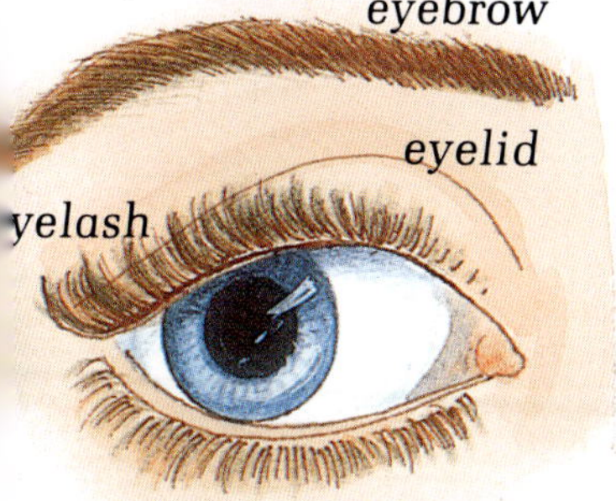

excursion an outing or journey

excuse 1 a reason for not doing something
2 to forgive

exercise 1 moving the body to keep fit such as running
2 to practise often

exhibition a show; a display

exile to send someone away from their country as a punishment

exit the way out

expand to grow bigger

expect to think something will happen

expedition a special journey to find something out

expensive costing a lot

experiment a test to find what will happen

expert a person with special knowledge or training

explain to describe the meaning of something

explode to burst into pieces with a loud noise

explore to look around a place thoroughly to find out more about it

export to send goods to be sold in other countries

express a very fast train or bus

expression a look on your face

extra more than usual

eye the part of the body that allows you to see

eyebrow hair above the eye

eyelash hair on the eyelid

eyelid the cover of skin used for opening or closing the eyes

eyesight the power to see

Ff

fabric cloth

face 1 the front part of the head
2 to look towards

fact something that is true or real

factory a place where things are made, usually by machinery

fade to lose colour

fail not to succeed

fairy

falcon

family

fang

farm

farmer

failure a try that wasn't a success

faint
1 not clear to see; dim
2 to lose one's senses and become unconscious

fair
1 light in colour
2 an open-air entertainment
3 less than good
4 honest; not taking sides

fairy a small, magical person in stories

faith a strong belief in somebody or something

faithful loyal; true; reliable

faithless disloyal; unreliable

fake copied; not real

falcon a kind of hawk, sometimes used for hunting

fall to drop down

false not true

family a father, mother and their children; close relatives

famine a great shortage of food

famous very well known

fan
1 something that makes a breeze
2 someone who very much likes a sports team, a singer, an actor etc

fang a long, sharp tooth

fantastic amazing, unbelievable

far a long way off

fare the price of a journey on a bus, train, taxi etc

farm land used for growing crops and raising animals

farmer a person who looks after a farm

fashion the style of clothes and other things popular at a certain time

fast
1 very quick
2 to go without food
3 firmly, tightly
(The climber held **fast** to the rope.)

fasten to hold together; to tie, join or close

fat
1 the greasy part of meat
2 plump and round

father a man who is a parent; dad, daddy

fault something that is wrong

favourite most liked

fawn 1

fawn 2

feast

feather

fern

ferry

fig

Ff

fawn 1 a young deer
2 a light yellowish-brown colour

fear a feeling of being in danger; to be afraid

fearless very brave; without fear

feast a very large meal, full of good things to eat

feather a part of a bird's covering

fee money paid for a service

feeble very weak

feed 1 to give food to
2 to eat

feel 1 to touch
2 to think
(I **feel** that our team can win.)

feet more than one foot

felt a thick kind of cloth

female a woman, or animal that can have babies

fence something put round a garden or field

fern a plant with long, feathery leaves but no flowers

ferry a boat to carry people and vehicles across water

fertile able to produce good crops

fertilizer a substance added to soil, to make it better for growing crops

festival a celebration or time of happiness, often with music, art, drama etc

few small in number

fibre a fine thread

fiction a made-up story

fiddle 1 a violin
2 to cheat

field 1 a piece of land used for crops or grazing
2 a place where sports are played

fierce wild and savage

fig a soft, sweet fruit, full of seeds

fight a struggle often using fists or weapons

figure 1 the shape of someone's body or an object
2 a number used in mathematics

file 1 a tool used for smoothing or wearing away hard material
2 a box or folder to keep papers in

fill to put into until there is no more room

filly a young female horse

film
1 material used for taking pictures in a camera
2 a moving picture shown on television or in a cinema
3 a very thin layer

filthy very dirty

fin one of the parts of a fish's body that helps it to swim

final the last; the end

finch one of several kinds of small, singing birds

find to come across what has been lost

fine
1 sunny and dry
2 very thin like a thread
3 money paid as a punishment
4 very good

finger one of the five long tips on your hand

fingerprint a pattern made by a finger

finish to end something

fir a tall, evergreen tree that has needle-like leaves

fire
1 something burning
2 to shoot a gun

fire-engine a vehicle that carries men and equipment for fighting fires

fire-escape a ladder or stairway used when a building is on fire

fire-extinguisher a container filled with chemicals that will put out a fire

fireman a person trained to put out fires

fire-station a building where fire-engines are kept

fireworks small explosives that give a colourful display or make a loud noise

firm
1 strong; steady
2 a business

first-aid help for people who are hurt

fish a swimming animal that lives in water

fisherman a person who catches fish

fist a tightly closed hand

fit
1 in good health
2 to be the right size and shape
3 suitable

fix
1 to make something firm
2 to repair or mend

flag a piece of cloth with an emblem or decoration on it

fleece

flint

florist

fluffy

flute

foal

flame		a tongue of fire
flap	*1*	to move up and down like wings
	2	something hanging down loosely
flash		a sudden, brief burst of light
flat	*1*	level; even
	2	a set of rooms on one floor
flavour		the taste of something
flea		a small, hopping insect without wings
flee		to run away in fear
fleece		the sheep's woolly coat
fleet	*1*	a number of ships sailing together
	2	a number of vehicles
flesh		the soft part of your body that covers the bones
flight	*1*	an aeroplane journey
	2	the movement of birds, insects etc
fling		to throw something
flint		a very hard stone
flip		to turn over quickly
flippers	*1*	the flat limbs of a seal, walrus or turtle
	2	rubber pieces, shaped like a seal's flipper, used by swimmers
float		to stay on the surface of the water
flock		a large group of birds or other animals
flood		an overflow of water from rivers, lakes or the sea
floor		the part of the room for walking on
florist		a person who sells flowers in a shop
flour		the fine white powder made by grinding grain
flower		the blossom of a plant
flu		short for influenza, a sickness that is like a very bad cold
fluffy		covered with soft hair or fur
fluid		a liquid
flute		a musical wind instrument made of wood or metal
flutter		to wave back and forth
fly	*1*	to move through the air
	2	a small, winged insect
foal		a young horse
foam		froth on the top of water
fog		thick mist or dirty air

Ff

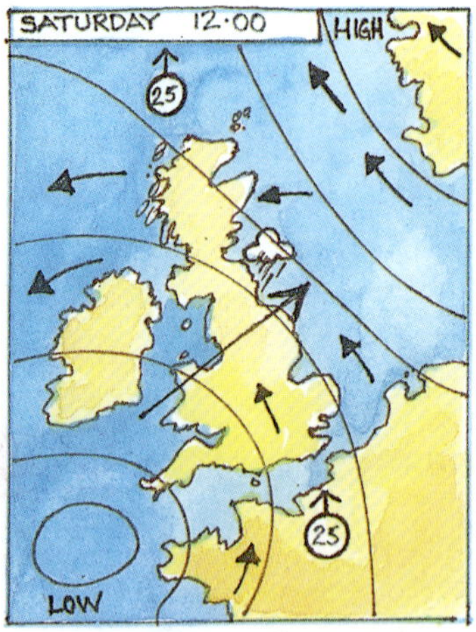

forecast

fork 1

fork 2

fort

fossil

fox

fold	*1* to double something over *2* a place where sheep are kept
follow	*1* to come after; to go after *2* to understand
food	what people, animals and plants eat to keep alive
fool	someone who is silly and stupid
foot	the part of each leg on which you stand and walk
football	*1* a game played by two teams *2* the ball used in the game
footprint	the mark of a foot on soft ground or on a clean floor
footsteps	the sounds made by the feet in walking
forbid	to tell someone not to do something
force	*1* strength; power *2* to make someone do something
forecast	to say what is likely to happen; a weather **forecast**
forehead	the part of the head between the hair and the eyes
foreign	belonging to another country
forest	a large area of land thickly covered with trees
forever	always
forget	not to remember
forgive	to let someone off when they have done wrong
fork	*1* a tool with prongs for eating or gardening *2* a place where a road or river divides
form	*1* a kind of bench on which we can sit *2* a printed paper with spaces to fill *3* a class in a school
fort	a building specially built to keep out the enemy
fortnight	two weeks
fortune	*1* either good or bad luck *2* a lot of money
fossil	the remains of an ancient animal or plant turned into stone
fountain	water shooting up into the air
fowl	a bird, usually of the farmyard
fox	a wild animal with a long bushy tail
fraction	a part of anything
fracture	a crack or break, usually of a bone
fragile	delicate, easily broken (This glass vase is **fragile.**)

frame

rog

frost

frown

fruit 1

fruit 2

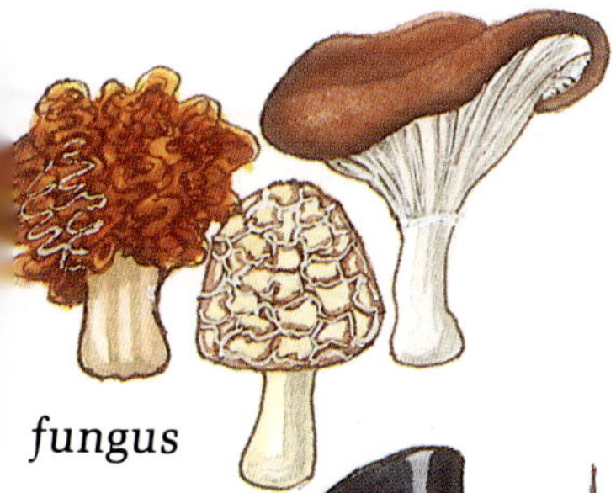
fungus

funnel 1

funnel 2

Ff

fragrant sweet-smelling

frame an edging for a picture or photograph

freckles light brown spots on the skin

free
1 not costing anything
2 able to do what you want to

freedom being free

freeze to turn into ice

freezer a machine which freezes food and keeps it fresh

freight the goods carried by a lorry, train, ship etc

frequent happening often

fresh
1 newly made; newly picked
2 not tired

fried cooked in hot fat

friend someone you know well and like

fright a scare; a sudden fear

frighten to make someone afraid

frog a small, jumping animal that lives in and out of water

front the part that faces forward; the beginning of something

frontier the boundary between two countries

frost powdered ice making a covering like snow

frown to wrinkle the forehead to show you are not pleased or you are puzzled

frozen so cold that water becomes ice

fruit
1 the part of any plant that holds the seeds
2 the juicy food from a plant

fry to cook in hot fat or oil

fuel anything that is burned to make heat

full unable to hold anything more

fun enjoyment; amusement; being happy

fungus a kind of plant that is without leaves, flowers or green colour

funnel
1 the chimney on a ship
2 an object to help you to pour liquid into a narrow opening

funny
1 amusing, making you laugh
2 strange; odd

fur the soft, hairy coat of some animals

furious very, very angry

furniture		things used in a house such as chairs, tables, beds etc
fuselage		the body of an aircraft
future		the time still to come

Gg

gadget		any useful tool or small machine
galaxy		a large group of stars
gale		a very strong wind
galleon		a Spanish sailing ship of olden times
gallery		a long room for displaying paintings
gallon		a measure of liquid equal to 4.5 litres
gallop		the fastest speed of a horse
game	*1*	a sport or pastime
	2	wild birds or animals that are hunted
gander		a male goose
gang		a set of people working together
gap		an opening or space
garage	*1*	a place where a car is kept
	2	a place where cars are repaired
garden		a piece of land where flowers, vegetables or fruit are grown
garlic		a strong-smelling plant bulb, used in cooking
garment		any piece of clothing
gas		an invisible air-like substance
gate		a hinged door in a wall or fence
gather		to collect together
gay		happy and full of fun
gaze		to look at long and steadily
gazelle		a small, fast antelope
gem		a precious stone
general	*1*	usual; ordinary
	2	a high-ranking officer in the army
generous		ready to give freely
gentle		quiet and kind; not rough
geography		the study of the earth and its people
gerbil		a small pet that looks like a mouse
germ		a tiny living thing that can cause disease and illness

gills

giraffe

glacier

glider

globe 1

globe 2

goat

Gg

get to obtain; to fetch

giant
1 anything that is much larger than normal
2 a huge person in fairy stories

gift something given; a present

giggle to laugh in a silly way

gills the openings in the head of a fish, used for breathing

ginger the root of a plant that grows in some hot countries

giraffe a tall African animal with a very long neck and legs

girl a female child

give to hand over

glacier a huge river of ice that moves very slowly

glad happy; pleased

glance a quick look

glare
1 a strong light
2 to stare at someone in an angry way

glass
1 a hard material that light can pass through
2 a drinking vessel

glasses spectacles worn to help people see better

glen a narrow, mountain valley

glide to move smoothly through air or water

glider a light aeroplane without an engine

glitter to shine with a bright, sparkling light

globe
1 anything in the shape of a ball
2 the earth, the world

gloomy dark and sad; miserable

glove a covering for your hand

glow to shine with a bright, warm colour

glue something to stick things together

gnat a small, flying insect that bites

gnaw to chew away at

gnome a storybook dwarf who lives underground

go to move away; to leave

goal
1 a place to aim at in games like football and hockey
(The forward aimed a shot at the **goal.**)
2 something you aim for
(Their **goal** was to raise enough money for a computer.)

goat a farm animal with horns and long hair

goblin a fairy tale elf who is mischievous

goggles

gondola

goose

gooseberry

gorilla

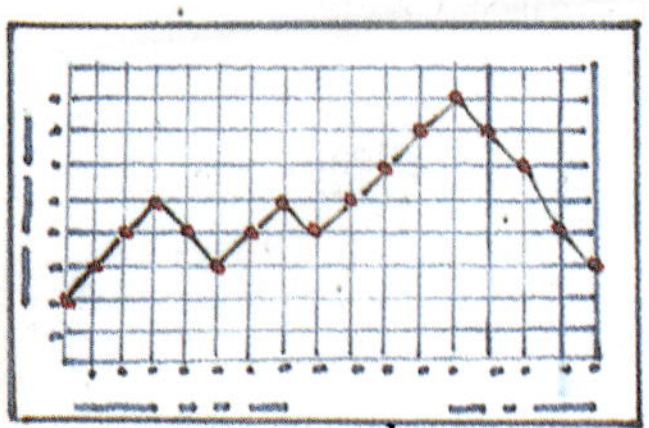
graph

grasshopper

god someone or something worshipped

goggles large glasses to protect the eyes

gold a very precious yellow metal

goldfish golden-red fish often kept as pets

golf an outdoor game played with special clubs and a small ball

gondola a long, narrow boat used on the canals of Venice

good
1 of a high standard
2 well behaved

goodbye what you say when you are going away

goose a large water bird

gooseberry a small fruit with a hairy skin

gorge a narrow valley between high cliffs

gorilla the largest and strongest ape

gossip to talk about other people saying things not always true; to chat

government the people chosen to rule or manage a country

gown a long dress

grab to snatch; to catch hold suddenly

gradual happening little by little

grain
1 the seed of corn, wheat, oats etc
2 a tiny piece of sand
3 the markings on wood

gram a very small weight

grandma grandmother; granny

grandpa grandfather; grandad

granite a very hard rock

grape a small, juicy fruit that grows in bunches on a vine

grapefruit a yellow fruit like a large orange and not so sweet

graph a chart, usually made of lines and dots, to show information

grasp to seize hold of firmly

grass a plant with thin, green leaves grown in fields and on lawns

grasshopper a jumping insect with long back legs

grass snake a small, harmless snake

grateful thankful

grave
1 a hole dug in the ground to bury a dead body
2 gloomy; serious

greenhouse

groom

grub

gravel small pebbles and stones

gravity the pull of the earth

gravy the juice that comes out of meat when it is cooked

graze
1 to eat grass
2 to scrape the skin

grease soft fat, or very thick oil

great
1 large
(A **great** cloud of smoke hung over the forest fire.)
2 important
(Lord Nelson was a **great** admiral.)

Gg

greedy wanting more than your share

green the colour of growing grass

greengrocer a person who sells fruit and vegetables

greenhouse a glass building where plants are grown

greet to say hello to someone; to welcome in a friendly way

grey a colour between black and white

grief great sadness; sorrow

grin to give a wide smile

grip to hold tightly

grit tiny pieces of stone

groan to make a sigh of disappointment or a deep sound of pain

grocer a person who sells food

groom a person who looks after horses

ground the earth we walk on

group a number of people or things together

grow
1 to get bigger
2 to raise plants

growl to make a deep, angry noise

grown-up an adult; a full-grown person

grub an insect when it has just hatched out of an egg

grumble to complain; to find fault

grunt the kind of sound a pig makes

guard
1 to look after or keep safe
2 someone who keeps watch and protects

guess to say without really knowing

guest a person who is visiting another's house

guide to show the way or lead someone

guinea-pig

guppy

gymkhana

guilty — having done something wrong

guinea-pig — a small, furry pet animal with no tail

guitar — a musical instrument with strings for plucking

gulf — a very large bay

gull — a grey and white bird found near the sea and inland waters

gulp — to swallow quickly

gum —
1 a kind of glue
2 the red flesh round your teeth

gun — a weapon that shoots bullets or shells

guppy — a very small, tropical fish

gutter — a channel to carry away waste water

gymkhana — a fete where horse jumping, racing and games take place

gymnasium — a room for body exercises and sports

gypsy/gipsy — a person belonging to a group of wandering people

Hh

haddock

hake

halibut

habit — something you do the same way all the time

haddock — a sea fish

hail — frozen drops of rain

hair — the covering which grows on the head and the skins of people and animals

haircut — the cutting and trimming of your hair

hairdresser — a person who cuts and takes care of people's hair

hake — a large sea fish

half — one of two equal parts of a whole

half-hour — thirty minutes

halibut — a large flatfish

hall —
1 a large room for meetings, concerts etc
2 an entrance space behind the door of a building

Hallowe'en — the night of October 31, when it was once believed that witches and ghosts appeared

halt — to stop

ham — meat from the leg of a pig

hamburger — a round piece of cooked minced beef eaten in a bread roll

hammer — a tool for hitting nails

hammock

hamster

handcuffs

harp
hatch 1

hatch 2

hazel

hammock		a hanging bed
hamper		a large container with a lid, often made of cane
hamster		a small, furry animal like a big mouse
hand		the palm and fingers at the lower end of your arm
handbag		a small bag often holding money, make-up, keys, a handkerchief etc
handcuffs		steel bracelets used to hold a prisoner's wrists together
handkerchief		a cloth for wiping your nose
handle	*1*	to touch, hold or move with your hands
	2	the part by which something is held
handlebars		the part of a bicycle held by the hands and used for steering
handsome		good-looking; attractive
hang		to fasten something so that is swings but does not fall
hangar		a large shed for aircraft
happen		to take place
happiness		gladness; joy; pleasure
happy		pleased; glad
harbour		a sheltered place for ships and boats
hard	*1*	firm, not soft
	2	difficult, not easy
hare		an animal like a large rabbit
harm		to damage; to hurt
harness		leather straps and fittings put on a horse
harp		a large musical instrument played by plucking its strings
harvest		the gathering of food crops
hat		a covering for the head
hatch	*1*	an opening in the deck of a ship
	2	to be born from an egg
hate		to dislike very much
haul		to drag; to pull
have		to own; to hold
hawk		a bird of prey with a strong, hooked beak and long, curved claws
hawthorn		a small tree with pink or white flowers and red berries
hay		grass cut and dried as food for animals
haze		slight mist or smoke
hazel		a small tree with nuts that can be eaten

hedgehog

helicopter

helm

helmet

herd

heron

head
1 the part of the body above the neck
2 the chief person

headache a pain in the head

headlights the main front lights of a car, lorry, bus etc

headquarters a main office

headteacher the person in charge of a school

heal to make or become well again

health how the body is, whether it is in good condition or not

healthy in good health; free from illness

heap a pile of things

hear to take in the sounds of things

heart the part of the body which pumps blood around it

heat warmth; hotness

heather a small, flowering plant that grows on moorland

heavens the sky

heavy having great weight; hard to lift

hectare a measurement for area

hedge a kind of fencing made of bushes, trees etc

hedgehog a small animal with sharp prickles on its back

heel the back part of your foot, under the ankle

heifer a young cow

height how high something is; the distance from top to bottom

helicopter an aircraft with rotors instead of wings; it can land and take off vertically and hover

hello a greeting

helm the tiller or wheel used to steer a boat or ship

helmet a covering to protect the head

help to assist; to aid

hen
1 a female chicken
2 any female bird

herb a plant whose leaves, stems or seeds are used to flavour food or to make medicine

herd a large group of animals together, such as cattle

here in this place

hermit a person who lives alone and stays away from other people

heron a long-legged wading bird, with a long beak and neck, that eats fish

herring

hexagon

hip 1

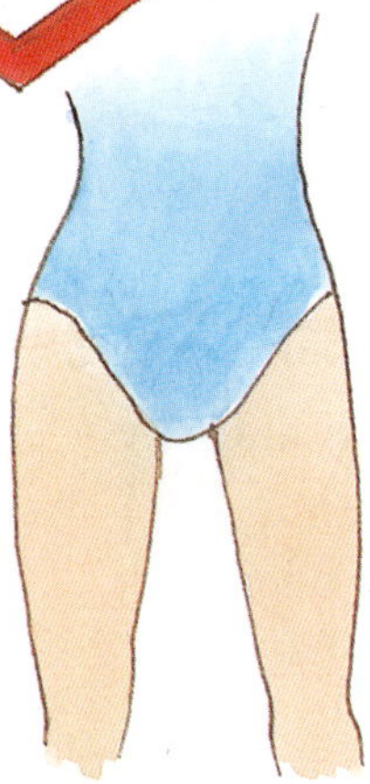

hip 2

hippopotamus

hive

holly

Hh

herring a small seafish which is often dried and smoked and called a kipper

hesitate to pause when you are unsure of what to do

hexagon a flat, six-sided figure

hibernate to sleep through the winter as bears and other animals do

hide
1 to put out of sight
2 an animal's skin

high a long way above the ground

high school a secondary school for older girls and boys

highway a main road

hike a long walk

hill a low mountain

Hindu a person who follows Hinduism, an Indian religion

hinge a joint on which a door or lid can move

hip
1 the place where the legs join the body
2 the fruit of the wild rose

hippopotamus a large, African water animal with thick skin

hiss a sound like an 'S'
(Geese and snakes **hiss** when they are angry.)

history the story of what happened in the past

hit
1 to strike or knock something
2 something popular like a record, a show etc

hive a place where bees live

hoard to collect and store things

hobby an interesting and useful pastime

hockey a team game played by two teams using curved sticks and a ball

hoe a long-handled tool for loosening the soil

hold
1 to have something in your hand
2 to contain
(Bottles **hold** liquids.)
3 the part of a ship that holds the cargo

hole an opening; a gap

holiday a time when there is no work or school; a period of rest and enjoyment

hollow empty; with nothing inside

holly an evergreen tree with prickly leaves and red berries

home a place where a person lives

honeycomb

hoof

horizon

horn 1

horn 2

hovercraft

homesick sad because you are away from home and miss your family and friends

homework school work done at home

honest always truthful and never stealing or cheating

honey a sweet, thick liquid made by bees

honeycomb where bees store honey inside a hive

honeymoon the holiday taken by a newly married couple

hood
1 a covering for the neck and head
2 a cover for a pram or an open car

hoof the hard part of the foot of some animals such as the horse, cow, sheep etc

hook a bent piece of metal for hanging things on, or catching fish

hop to jump up and down on one foot

hope to wish that something would happen

horizon the line where sea and sky, or earth and sky seem to meet

horn
1 hard bone sticking out of animal's head
2 a musical instrument played by blowing

hornet a large wasp that stings

horrible very unpleasant; terrible; awful

horror great fear and shock

horse a large animal with hooves, used for riding

horseshoe an iron shoe worn by a horse on each hoof

hosepipe a tube through which water flows

hospital a building where ill or hurt people are cared for by doctors and nurses

hot very warm; full of heat

hot dog a warm sausage inside a roll

hotel a building where people pay to stay

hour a length of time equal to sixty minutes

house a building in which people live

housework jobs done at home such as cooking, cleaning, washing, ironing etc

hovercraft a land or water vehicle that moves on a cushion of air

how in which way

howl a long, loud cry
(Dogs sometimes **howl** in a thunder-storm.)

hug to hold tightly in the arms

humming-bird

husky

hyacinth

hyena

iceberg

huge	enormous in size (The elephant is a **huge** animal.)
hull	the frame or body of a ship
hum	to make a noise like a bee
human	having to do with people, not animals
humid	moist, damp
humming bird	a small, brightly-coloured bird whose wings flap so quickly they make a humming sound
humorous	funny
hump	a large bulge or bump, usually on the back
hungry	needing or wanting food
hunt	*1* to look very carefully for something *2* to try to catch wild animals
hurricane	a storm with a very powerful wind and heavy rain
hurry	to move very quickly
hurt	to cause pain or harm to someone
husband	a married man
hush	to keep quiet
husky	a strong dog, used in very cold places to pull a sledge
hut	a small, wooden building
hutch	a box for a pet rabbit to live in
hyacinth	a garden flower grown from a bulb
hyena	a dog-like animal with a laughing call
hymn	a song of praise
hypermarket	a very large supermarket

Ii

ice	frozen water
iceberg	a mountain of ice floating in the sea
ice-cream	a flavoured cream, sweetened and frozen
ice-skate	a skate with a blade that glides on the ice
icicle	a pointed stick of hanging ice
icing	a sweet covering put on cakes
idea	a thought in the head
identical	exactly the same
idiot	a very stupid or foolish person
idle	lazy, not wanting to work

igloo

iguana

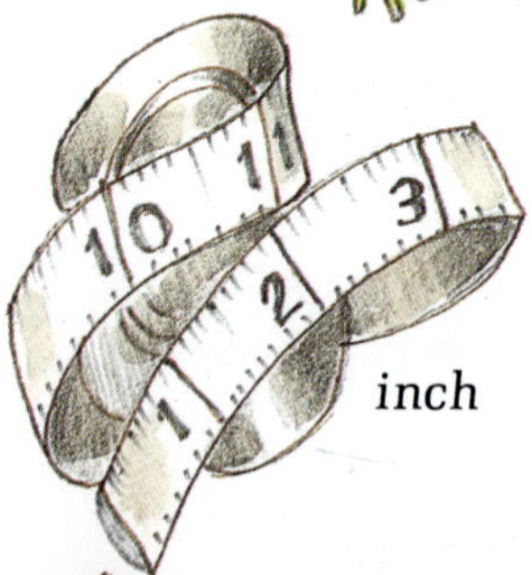

inch

inn

insect

igloo an Eskimo house made of blocks of hard snow

iguana a large, climbing lizard

ill not well; in poor health

illustrate to explain something by drawing pictures

imagine to picture a thing in your mind

imitate to copy; to do the same as someone else

immediately at once

immense huge; very big

impatient finding it hard to wait

import to bring goods from another country into this country

important meaning a lot; of great value

impossible not able to be done

improve to make better, or become better

inch a measurement of length equal to about 2.5cm

increase to make larger or greater

index a list, in alphabetical order, at the end of a book

indoors inside a building

infant a very young child

influenza an illness often called flu

inhabit to live in a place

injection to put medicine into your body with a needle

injure to hurt; to harm

ink a coloured liquid used for writing and printing

inland away from the coast

inn a small hotel where people may eat and sleep; a public house

innings when you bat at cricket, rounders or baseball

innocent having done nothing wrong; not guilty

inquire to ask about something; to try to find out

insect a small animal with six legs

inside the part within; not outside

inspect to examine very closely

instalment
1 a part of a story
2 a payment towards the full cost of anything

instead in place of

instep the middle of the foot

instruct to tell someone how to do something

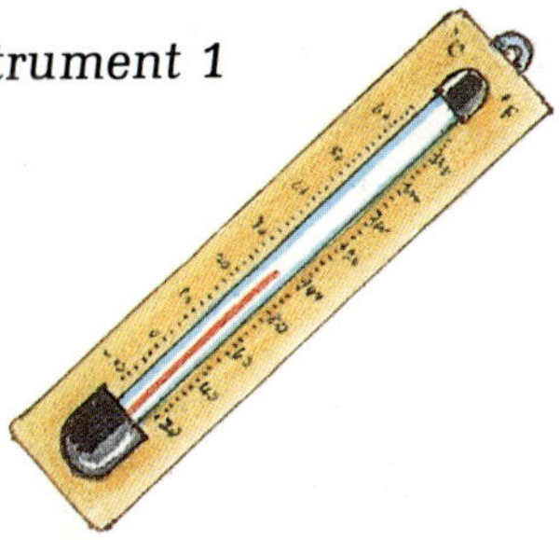
instrument 1

instrument 2

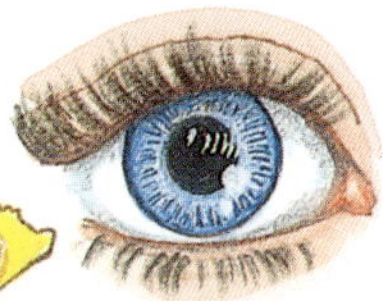
iris 1

iris 2

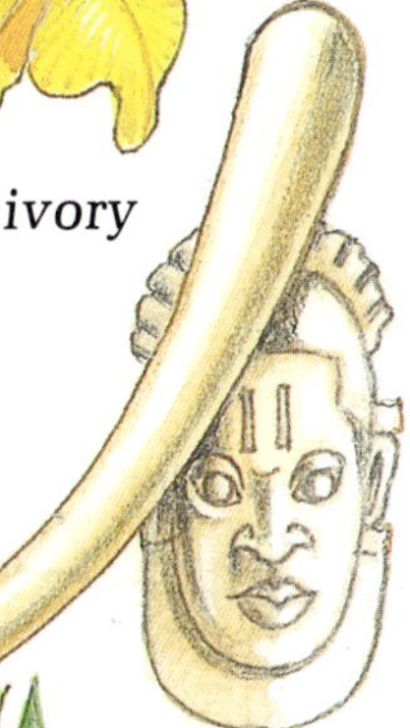
ivory

ivy

jaguar

instrument
1 a tool
(A thermometer is an **instrument** that tells how hot or cold it is.)
2 anything that makes music

intelligent quick at learning; clever

interest something you enjoy doing or want to learn more about

interfere to get in the way; to meddle in other people's business

international having to do with two or more nations

interrupt to break into what someone is saying or doing

into to the inside of
(The children went **into** the classroom.)

introduce to say the names of people when they meet for the first time

invade to enter a country by force

invalid a person who is weak from an illness

invent to plan or make something for the first time

invisible not able to be seen

invitation asking someone to come to a place

iris
1 the coloured part of your eyeball
2 a garden flower

iron
1 a strong, hard metal
2 a tool, when heated, for smoothing clothes

Islam the religion of the followers of Mohammed

island a piece of land with water all round it

itch a tickling feeling of the skin

ivory the hard, white material of an elephant's tusk

ivy a climbing plant, often having shiny, green leaves

Jj

jab to poke; to push something pointed

jack a tool for lifting heavy objects

jackal a wild animal that looks like a dog

jacket a short coat

jagged with rough, torn edges

jaguar a wild animal like a leopard, but much heavier, living in South America

jail a prison

jay

jellyfish

jewellery

jockey

jam	*1* a food made from fruit boiled with sugar until it is thick *2* a tight crowd of people or traffic (We were in a traffic **jam** for two hours.)
jar	a container made of pottery or glass
javelin	a light spear thrown by hand
jaw	one of the two bones of the mouth from which the teeth grow
jay	a brightly coloured bird which makes a loud noise
jazz	a lively kind of music
jealous	wanting what someone else has
jeans	strong cotton trousers, usually blue
jeep	a small, powerful type of car able to travel over rough country
jelly	a food made from fruit juice, sugar and water; it wobbles when it has set
jellyfish	a small sea animal that has a soft, jelly-like body
jerk	a quick tug or movement
jersey	a knitted garment
jet	*1* a narrow stream of liquid or gas forced through a small hole *2* a type of aircraft pushed forward by jets of hot gas
jewel	any precious stone such as a diamond, ruby etc
jewellery	rings, bracelets, necklaces etc
jigsaw	a puzzle picture made by fitting pieces together
job	work; anything a person has to do
jockey	a person who rides horses in races
jog	to run at a slow pace
join	*1* to fasten together *2* to become a member of a group (Sarah will soon **join** the Girl Guides.)
joiner	someone who works with wood
joint	*1* the point where two things are joined together *2* a piece of meat
joke	a story which makes people laugh
jolly	full of fun; happy
journalist	a person who writes for a newspaper
journey	a trip from one place to another
joy	feeling of great happiness

juggler

junk 1

junk 2

kangaroo

key 1

key 2

judge 1 a person who is in charge of a court of law
2 to decide who or which is best

judo a Japanese form of wrestling

jug a container for liquids

juggler a person who is skilled at balancing things and keeping them moving in the air

juice the liquid in fruits or vegetables, and in meat

jumble a muddle; a mixed-up mess

jump to leap into the air with both feet off the ground

junction where two or more roads, lines, wires etc, meet

jungle land in hot, wet places that is thickly covered with trees, shrubs etc

junior someone who is younger

junk 1 worthless rubbish
2 a Chinese sailing ship

just 1 fair
2 exactly right
3 a moment ago

juvenile a young person

Kk

kangaroo a jumping, Australian animal that carries its young in a pouch

karate a Japanese form of self-defence

kayak an Eskimo canoe

keen 1 sharp like the blade of a knife
2 interested; eager to do a thing

keep to hold; to hold on to something for yourself

keeper a person who looks after things, such as animals in a zoo

kennel a shelter for a dog

kerb the edge of a path or pavement

kernel the inside part of a nut, the part you eat

kettle a metal container used for boiling liquid

key 1 a tool to open a lock
2 one of the parts pressed down with the fingers on a piano or a computer

kick to hit with your foot

kick-off the start of a football game

kid a young goat

Jj Kk

King 1

king 2

kingfisher

kiwi

knight 1

knight 2

kidnap	to take someone away by force
kill	to put to death
kilogram	a measure of weight; a thousand grams
kilometre	a measure of distance; a thousand metres
kilt	a pleated skirt often worn in Scotland
kind	*1* helpful, friendly to other people *2* a sort or type of thing
king	*1* a male ruler of a country *2* a piece in a game of chess
kingfisher	a small, colourful bird which lives near water and eats fish
kiosk	*1* a public telephone box *2* a small, open hut where things are sold
kipper	a smoked herring
kiss	to touch with the lips
kit	*1* a set of tools or materials needed to do a certain job *2* a set of jerseys, shorts, socks etc for certain games
kitchen	a room where food is prepared and cooked
kite	a very light frame covered with material for flying at the end of a long string
kitten	a young cat
kiwi	a New Zealand bird with very short wings that cannot fly
knee	the joint in the middle of your leg
kneel	to go down on your knees
knife	a cutting tool, a sharp blade fitted with a handle
knight	*1* a man wearing armour who used to fight on horseback *2* a piece in a game of chess
knit	to weave wool or other material with needles
knob	the round handle of a door or drawer
knock	*1* to tap or rap with the knuckles *2* to hit or bump into
knot	*1* a fastening made by tying together pieces of string or rope *2* a mark in a piece of wood *3* a measure of the speed of ships
know	*1* to be sure; to understand *2* to remember somebody
knuckle	a joint in a finger

koala

kookaburra

labrador

ladybird

lagoon

larva

lasso

koala a small, furry 'bear' from Australia; it lives in eucalyptus trees

kookaburra an Australian bird with a cry like laughter

Ll

label a small piece of paper or card for fastening on to parcels

laboratory a place where experiments in science are carried out

Labrador a large black or gold coloured dog often used as a guide dog for the blind

lace
1 a material made from thin threads that form a pattern
2 something to tie up a shoe

ladder wooden or metal steps for climbing

lady a woman

ladybird a small, flying beetle, red or orange, with black spots

lagoon a shallow, salt-water lake

lake a large area of water with land all around

lamb a young sheep

lame unable to walk properly

lamp a device that provides light

lamp-post a tall post which holds a street light

land
1 ground; soil
2 the part of the earth not covered by water
3 to reach the earth from the air or sea

landing
1 a platform on a staircase
2 an aircraft's coming down to earth

lane a narrow road or a wide pathway

language the words used by people when they speak or write

lantern a glass case with a light inside

lap
1 using the tongue to drink, as a cat or dog does
2 once round a track in a race
3 part of a sitting person

larch a tall, evergreen tree with cones and needle-like leaves

lard animal fat used for cooking

larder a room with shelves for keeping food

large big; great in size

larva the early form of an insect

lasso a rope with a loop at the end, used for catching cattle

last
1 coming after all the others
2 to go on for a long time

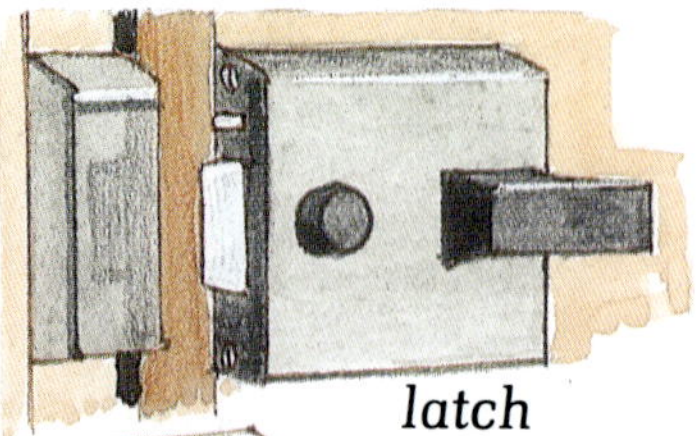
latch

launch 1

launch 2

launch 3

lawnmower

layer

leaf 1

leaf 2

latch a fastening for a door

late coming after the usual time; not early

laugh the sound you make when you see or hear something funny

launch
1 a motor boat
2 to slide a ship into the water
3 to send a rocket into space

launching-pad a base from which rockets are launched

laundry
1 clothes needing washing
2 a place where clothes are washed and ironed

lava hot, melted rock flowing from a volcano

lavatory a toilet

law a rule made by a government

lawn grass kept cut and tidy

lawn-mower a machine used for cutting grass

lawyer someone who has studied the law and advises other people

lay
1 to put something down carefully
2 to produce eggs

layer a thickness; a coating

lazy idle; not wanting to work

lead (like led) a heavy, grey metal

lead (like feed)
1 a strap used to hold a dog
2 to go in front; to show the way

leader someone who goes in front and shows the way or takes charge

leaf
1 one of the small, green flat parts of a plant
2 a page of a book

leak a crack or hole that lets liquid or gas escape

lean
1 thin
2 having little fat
3 to rest against something

leap to jump

leap year every fourth year, when February has 29 days instead of 28

learn to find out; to get to know

least the smallest in size or amount

leather an animal's skin specially treated and used for shoes, handbags, belts etc

leave
1 to go away from
2 to let something stay where it is

ledge

leek

lemon

leopard

rarian

library 1

library 2

lifeguard

ledge		a narrow shelf
leek		a vegetable which tastes like an onion, with a white stem and green leaves
left		the opposite to right
leg	*1*	a limb of the body
	2	one of the supports for a chair or table
leisure		spare time
lemon		a yellow fruit with a sour taste
lemonade		a fizzy drink made from lemon juice
lend		to let someone use something of yours for a time
length		the distance from end to end
lens		special curved glass used in spectacles, cameras, telescopes etc
leopard		a large, spotted animal of the cat family found in Asia and Africa
leotard		a tight, one-piece garment worn by dancers, gymnasts and others
less		smaller; not as much
let		to allow
letter	*1*	one of the symbols of the alphabet
	2	a written message put in an envelope and sent to someone
letter-box		the opening in the door for a postman to push letters through
lettuce		a green vegetable used in salads
level		smooth and flat; not sloping
lever		a handle to a machine, such as a gear-lever
liar		someone who does not tell the truth
librarian		a person who works in a library
library	*1*	a collection of books
	2	a building where books are kept
lick		to wet with your tongue
lid		a cover for a container
lie	*1*	something that is not true
	2	to rest, stretched flat
life		the time you are alive
lifeguard		a trained swimmer who watches to see that swimmers are safe
lift	*1*	to raise
	2	an apparatus in a building for taking people and goods from one floor to another

Ll

light
1 brightness
2 not heavy; easy to lift
3 to set on fire

lighthouse a tower with a flashing light which warns ships of danger

lightning a flash of electricity in the sky during a thunderstorm

like
1 similar to; the same as
2 to be fond of

likeness a copy
(The photograph is a good **likeness** of you.)

lilac a small tree that has sweet-smelling blossom

lily a tall garden flower that grows from a bulb

limb
1 an arm or a leg
2 a branch of a tree

lime
1 a greenish fruit that looks like a lemon
2 a white powder made from limestone

limit the end of something; the edge
(The cliffs mark the **limit** of our walk.)

limp
1 to walk lamely; to hobble
2 hanging loosely; not stiff

limpet a small shellfish which clings to rocks

line
1 a long thin mark
2 a piece of rope, string or cord
3 a row
(A long **line** of people were waiting to buy tickets.)

linen
1 cloth made from flax
2 such things as towels, sheets, table-cloths etc

link one of the rings in a chain

lion a large wild animal of the cat family found in parts of Asia and Africa

lip one of the two pink, fleshy edges of your mouth

lipstick make-up used to colour the lips

liquid something that will flow, like water.

list a number of items written one after the other

listen to try to hear

litre a measure of liquids equal to about 1¾ pints

litter
1 a number of animals all born together
2 rubbish lying about

little small; not much

live
1 to be alive
2 to make a home somewhere

lizard

llama

lobster

lock 1

lock 2

loom

lively full of life and energy

liver a vital part of the inside of your body

living-room the main room in a house

lizard a reptile with four short legs and a long-tail

llama a large South American animal with long hair

load
1 something carried
2 to put a bullet or shell into a gun

loaf bread shaped and baked in one large piece

lobster a large shellfish with eight legs and two claws

local nearby; in your area

loch a Scottish word for lake

lock
1 a fastening for a door or box
2 a place in a canal where ships can be raised or lowered

locomotive a railway engine

locust an insect like a grasshopper found in Asia and Africa, which flies in swarms from place to place often destroying crops

loft a space under the roof of a building

log
1 a sawn-off part of a tree trunk or branch
2 the diary of a ship's or aircraft's journey

lollipop a large sweet on a stick

lonely alone; with nobody else there

long
1 to want very much
2 far from one end to the other

look to watch; to see

loom a machine for weaving cloth

loose slack; not fastened tightly

lorry a large motor vehicle for carrying heavy loads

lose
1 to put something where you cannot find it
2 to be beaten

lost cannot be found; unable to find the way

lot a large number

loud noisy

loudspeaker a piece of equipment for making live or recorded sounds louder

lounge
1 a sitting room in a house or hotel
2 to sit about in a lazy manner

love to be very fond of

lovely beautiful; delightful to look at

luggage

lumberjack

lynx

mackerel

magnet
magpie
maize

low — 1 not high; close to the ground
2 the sound made by cattle

lower — 1 to pull or let down
(Will you **lower** the blind to keep out the sun?)
2 not as high
(The water in the lake is **lower** than it was last summer.)

loyal — reliable; faithful and true

luck — something good or bad that happens by chance

luggage — the suitcases and bags we need when travelling

lukewarm — not too hot and not too cold; slightly warm

lumberjack — a man who cuts down trees

lump — 1 a swelling on the skin
2 a piece of anything

lunar — having to do with the moon

lunch — a meal in the middle of the day

lungs — the parts of the body used for breathing

lynx — a kind of wild cat

Mm

macaroni — hollow tubes made of a mixture of flour paste, often eaten with cheese

machine — a device that makes things, or does some particular job

mackerel — a silvery fish that lives in ocean waters

mackintosh — a coat that keeps the rain out

mad — ill in your mind; crazy

magazine — a thin book containing pictures and stories or articles

magic — the use of clever tricks to make impossible things seem to happen

magician — someone who performs magic tricks

magnet — a bar of iron or steel that attracts or draws pieces of metal towards it

magnifying glass — a lens that makes things look bigger than they really are

magpie — a large black and white bird like a crow

mail — letters, cards, parcels sent by post

main — most important; chief

maize — a kind of corn with large seeds

majesty — a title given to a king or queen

major — 1 an officer in the army
2 of much importance

mallet

mammoth

ane

Maoris

maple

majority the greatest number in a group
(The **majority** of my friends walk to school.)

make
1 a kind; a brand
(What **make** is your car?)
2 to build; to construct something
(Many boys like to **make** model aircraft.)
3 to force somebody to do something
(**Make** the dog sit down!)

make-up powder, cream, lipstick etc put on the face

malaria an illness carried by the bite of certain types of mosquito

male a boy; a man

mallet a kind of hammer made of wood or rubber

mammal any animal that feeds its young with its own milk

mammoth a large extinct kind of elephant

man a grown-up male person

manage
1 to take charge and look after
2 to be able to do something

manager a person in charge

mane the long hair on the neck of an animal, such as a horse, giraffe, lion etc

Mm

manger a long feeding box for horses and cattle

mankind all people; the human race

manner
1 the way something is done
2 the way some behave

mansion a very large house

manure animal droppings and straw put on the ground to help plants grow better

many a great number; plenty

Maoris the original people of New Zealand

map a drawing of the earth's surface showing the shape of countries, positions of towns and rivers, height of land etc

maple a type of tree

marble
1 a small, glass ball used as a toy
2 a hard stone used in making buildings and statues

march
1 to walk in step with others
2 a piece of music people can march to

mare a female horse

margarine a spread made from vegetable oils, used instead of butter

margin space at the sides, top and bottom of written or printed pages

marina

mask

matador

mayor

marina a small harbour for pleasure boats

mark
1 a sign put on something
2 a spot, stain or scratch
3 a score on a test or piece of work

market a busy place where things are bought and sold, often from stalls in the open

marmalade a type of jam, usually made from oranges

maroon a dark red colour

marriage
1 a wedding
2 living together as husband and wife

marry to become husband and wife

marsh wet, swampy ground

marvellous wonderful; surprising and amazing

mascot an animal, person or thing supposed to bring good luck

mask a covering for the face

mason a person who builds with stone

mass a great lump or quantity

mast a pole used to hold up sails or flags

mat
1 a small rug to wipe your feet on
2 something put under hot dishes

matador a bullfighter

match
1 a small, thin stick with a tip that lights when it is struck
2 a game between two sides
3 to sort by size, shape or colour

material what something is used for or made of

mathematics the study of numbers and measurement

matinée an afternoon performance in a theatre or cinema

matter anything that can be seen and touched

mattress the thick, soft part of the bed on which we sleep

may to be possible

maybe perhaps
(**Maybe** it will rain tomorrow.)

mayor the chief person of a city or town

meadow a field of grass or hay in the country

meal the food which we eat each day at a certain time

mean
1 to intend to do something
2 selfish; unkind

measles a catching illness when the body is covered with small, red spots

melon

menu

meteor

meter

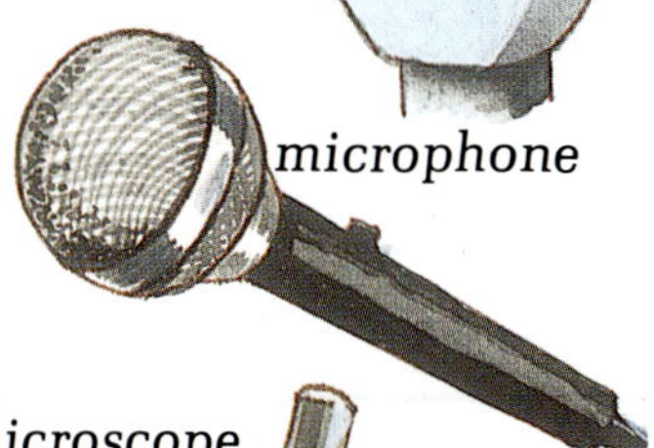

microphone

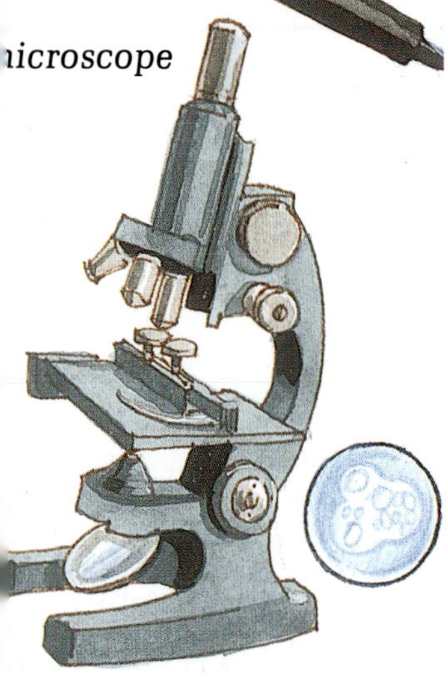

microscope

measure to find the size or amount

meat animal flesh used for food

mechanic a person who repairs machines

medal a flat piece of metal that is given as a prize or a reward

medicine a liquid, pill or other substance we take to make us better when we are ill

meet to come together

meeting the coming together of people to talk or listen to someone

melody a tune

melon a large, sweet juicy fruit

melt to change into a liquid by using heat

member someone who belongs to a club or group

memory the power of remembering things

men males

mend to repair something that is broken

menu a list of all the foods served in a café or restaurant

meow the sound that a cat makes

mercury a heavy, silvery liquid metal

mermaid a fairy-tale sea creature who has a fish's tail instead of legs and a woman's body

merry laughing; happy; full of fun

mess a dirty or untidy state of things

message news sent from one person to another

metal material such as iron, steel, gold, copper etc

meteor a large rock that falls from space towards earth; a shooting star

meter an instrument that measures amounts and times

method a way of doing something

metre a measure of length

microphone an instrument which picks up sounds to make them louder

microscope an instrument that makes tiny things look large

midday twelve o'clock in the daytime; noon

middle the point that is half-way between two things

midnight twelve o'clock at night

might
1 to be possible
2 power; strength

mill 1

migrate to move to another place or country (Some birds **migrate** to warmer lands in winter.)

mild
1 gentle; not strong
2 neither hot nor cold

mile a measure of distance equal to about 1610 metres

milk the white liquid that female mammals produce to feed their young

milkshake a drink of milk and flavouring of fruit, chocolate etc

mill 2

mill
1 a place where grain is ground into flour
2 a factory making cloth or steel

million a thousand thousands; 1,000,000

millionaire a very rich person who has at least a million pounds

mime to act out a story using actions but no words

mince to chop into very small pieces

mincemeat a mixture of chopped nuts, fruits and spices

mine
1 belonging to me
2 a place from which coal, iron or other minerals are obtained

miner

miner a man who works in a mine

mineral anything dug out of earth such as coal, rock, diamonds etc

miniature very small

minister someone who takes services in a church or chapel

minor not very important

mint
1 a plant with a strong scent
2 a place where money is made

minus less than; the sign −

minute (say minit) a measure of time

minute (say mynute) very small

miracle a marvellous and unexpected happening

mirror

mirror a glass in which you can see yourself

misbehave to behave badly

mischief silly things done to annoy or harm others

miser a person who has a lot of money but does not like spending it

miserable unhappy; sad

Miss a word used in front of a young lady's name

miss
1 fail to hit, catch or find
2 to be lonely for someone who is away from you

mistletoe

moat

moccasins

mole 1

ole 2

missile		a weapon which is thrown or fired
mission		a special job or task
mist		a thin fog or haziness in the air
mistake		something that is wrong; a fault; an error
mistletoe		a plant with white berries, used as a Christmas decoration
mittens		gloves that cover four fingers together, and the thumb separately
mix		to stir together
moan		a low groaning sound, often showing pain
moat		a wide ditch with water round a castle
mob		a noisy and dangerous crowd of people
moccasins		shoes made from soft leather
mock		to make fun of
model	*1*	a small copy of something
	2	a person who wears clothes and shows them to people who may buy them
modern		up-to-date
module		part of a space vehicle
moist		damp; slightly wet
mole	*1*	a small, furry animal that makes tunnels under the ground
	2	a small, dark spot on the skin
moment		a very short space of time
monastery		a building where monks live and work
money		coins and paper notes used to buy things
mongrel		a dog of mixed breed
monk		a holy man who lives in a monastery
monkey		a small ape
monster		a strange and frightening creature in a fairy story
month		one of the twelve parts of a year, eg January
monument		a statue or building put up in memory of someone or some event
moo		the long, low sound a cow makes
mood		the way that you feel at a certain time
moon		the body which moves round the earth once every 28 days, and can be seen in the sky at night
moonbeam		a ray of moonlight

moose

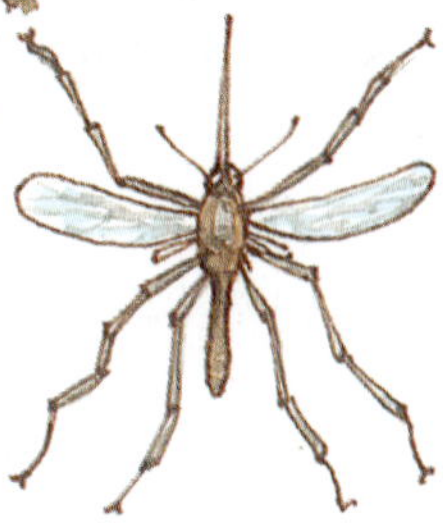
mosquito

moss

moth

mountaineer

mule

moor — *1* a large, open area of rough ground where very little grows
2 to fasten a boat to stop it drifting away

moose — a large animal like a deer which lives in Canada and parts of USA

mop — material at the end of a pole, for wiping floors

more — greater; extra

morning — the part of the day before noon or midday

mosquito — a small, two winged insect which bites

moss — a smooth, green plant that grows on damp trees and stones

most — the greatest number; the largest quantity

motel — a hotel for travelling motorists

moth — a flying insect like a butterfly, usually seen at night

mother — a woman who has a child or children

motor — an engine to make things work or move

motorboat — a boat powered by an engine

motorcycle — a two-wheeled vehicle powered by a motor

motorist — a person who travels by car

motorway — a special, wide road for faster traffic

mountain — a very high hill

mountaineer — someone who climbs mountains

mouse — a small, furry animal with a pointed nose and a long tail

moustache — hair that grows above a man's top lip

mouth — the opening in your face for eating and talking

move — to go from one place to another

mow — to cut grass with a machine

much — a large amount

mud — soft, wet soil

muddle — a mix up; a jumble

mug — a large drinking cup

mule — an animal that is half donkey and half horse

multiply — to make a number so many times greater

mum — a short way of saying mother

mummy — *1* a child's name for mother
2 a dead body treated with chemicals and wrapped in cloths to prevent decay

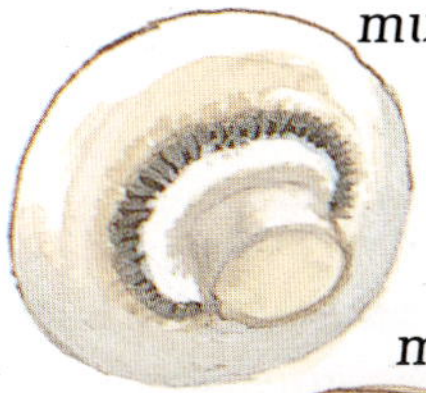
mushroom

mussel

muzzle 1

muzzle 2

nail 1

nail 2

narcissus

mumps	an illness that gives you a swollen neck and a sore throat
munch	to chew in a noisy way
murder	to kill someone on purpose
murmur	*1* to speak very softly *2* a soft low sound
muscles	the parts of the body which help us to move the limbs
museum	a building in which interesting and ancient objects can be seen
mushroom	a small plant, shaped like an umbrella, that can be eaten
music	pleasing sounds and notes made by playing instruments and singing
musician	someone who plays music
mussel	a shellfish with a narrow, black shell
mustard	a yellow paste which adds a hot flavour to food
mutter	to speak or grumble in a low voice
mutton	the meat from sheep
muzzle	*1* the nose and jaws of an animal *2* a covering for the mouth of an animal to stop it biting
mystery	something very strange and hard to understand

Mm Nn

Nn

nail	*1* a pointed piece of metal for joining two pieces of wood *2* the thin, hard layer at the end of a finger or toe
naked	bare; without clothes
name	what a person or thing is called
nap	a short sleep
narcissus	a spring flower grown from a bulb
narrow	not wide; not far across
nasty	not good to taste; not pleasant to see
nation	a country, or the people of a country
native	someone born in a certain place or country (Kim is a **native** of Australia.)
natural	as nature made it; not made by man
nature	living things; people, plants and animals
naughty	badly behaved
navigate	to guide or plan the route of a ship or aircraft
navy	a country's warships and sailors
near	not far away; close to

necklace

nest

netball

newt

nightingale

nomad

nearly almost

neat clean and tidy

necessary something that we must have or must be done (Sleep is **necessary** for good health.)

neck the part of the body that joins the head to the shoulders

necklace a string of beads or jewels worn around the neck

need to want badly

needle a thin, pointed object used for sewing and knitting

neigh the noise a horse makes

neighbour someone who lives near you

neither not one or the other

nephew a son of your brother or sister

nervous timid, easily frightened

nest a place where a bird lays its eggs

net thread woven into a pattern to leave openings

netball a game where a ball is thrown through a high ring

never not at any time

new just made; never used

news telling about something which has just happened

newspaper a daily or weekly paper with news, stories, pictures and advertisements

newt a small animal like a lizard that can live in or out of water

next nearest; touching; the one following

nibble to eat something in tiny bites

nice pretty; friendly; pleasant

nickname a name people use instead of your proper name

niece the daughter of a sister or brother

night the time when it is dark, between sunset and sunrise

nightingale a small, European song-bird

nimble quick and light on the feet

nobody no one

noise a sound, sometimes unpleasant

nomad a member of a wandering tribe

none not one; not any

nonsense silliness; stupid talk

nook a quiet little corner

north

nursery 1

nursery 2

oasis

oats

noon		twelve o'clock midday
normal		usual; ordinary
north		the direction opposite the sun at midday; the opposite to south
nose		the part of the face through which you breathe and smell
nostril		one of the two openings in the nose
note	*1*	a short message
	2	a musical sound
	3	a piece of paper money
nothing		not a single thing
notice	*1*	to see something
	2	a piece of information to be read
nought		the number 0; zero; nothing
novel	*1*	a long story in book form
	2	new, sometimes strange
now		at present; at this moment
nudge		to push someone with your elbow to get his or her attention
nuisance		anything which annoys us or stops us from getting on with what we are doing
numb		without any feeling (Sandy sat on her foot so long that it became **numb**.)
number	*1*	a word or figure that tells how much
	2	several (There are a **number** of children not listening.)
nun		a holy woman who lives in a convent or a nunnery
nurse		a person trained to look after the sick, the old and the very young
nursery	*1*	a room or building where young children play and sleep
	2	a place where young plants are grown
nut	*1*	a dry fruit or seed with a hard shell
	2	a piece of metal with a hole in the centre, for screwing onto a bolt
nylon		a strong, man-made thread

Oo

oak	a large tree of hard wood; its fruit is the acorn
oar	a pole with a flat end to row a boat
oasis	a place in the desert where there are trees and water
oats	a cereal used for making porridge

Nn Oo

observatory

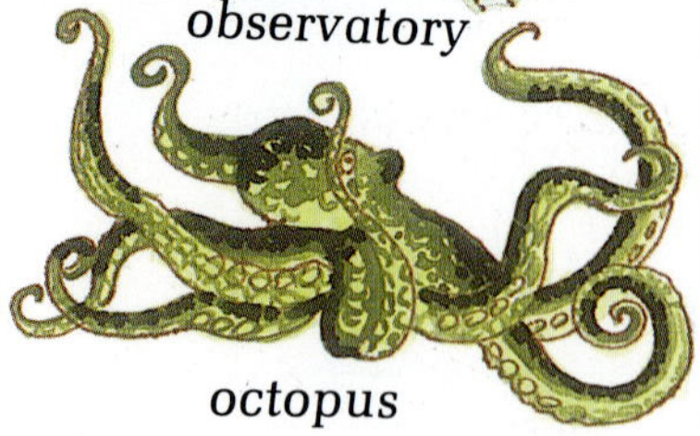
octopus

office

ogre

Olympic Games

obedient doing as you are told

obey to do as you are told

object
1 something that you can see and touch
2 to grumble about; to disagree with

oblong a four-sided figure that is longer than it is wide

observatory a building where there are telescopes for studying the stars

observe to watch carefully

obstacle something in the way

obtain to get

occupation the work that somebody does for a living

occupy to fill in space; to live in

occur to take place; to happen

ocean a large sea, such as the Pacific

o'clock the time shown by the clock

octopus a sea creature with eight arms or tentacles

odd
1 not even in number; not able to be divided exactly by two
2 strange; peculiar

off
1 away from
(The cat knocked a vase **off** the table.)
2 away
(The dog ran **off**.)

offer
1 to say that we are ready to do something
2 to hold out a thing for someone to take or refuse

office a room or building where paperwork is done

often many times

ogre in fairy tales, a monster who frightens people

oil a greasy liquid obtained from underground and plants

ointment a healing paste to put on sores and cuts

old
1 of great age; not new
2 having lived for a certain time

old-fashioned out-of-date; not modern

olive a small oily fruit

Olympic Games athletic contests held every four years in a different country

once
1 one time
2 in the past

onion a vegetable like a bulb and with a strong taste

ɔpera

orange 1

orange 2

ɾchard

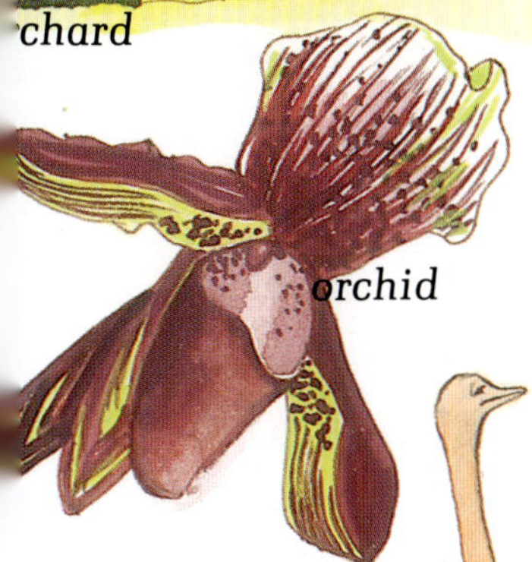

ɾrchid

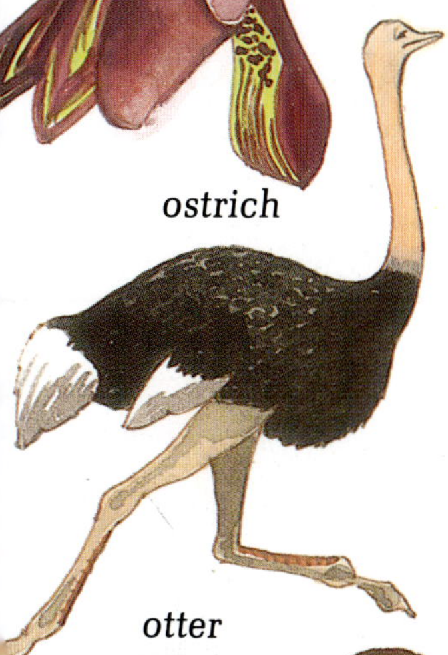

ostrich

otter

only		by itself; no more
open		not shut; not covered over
opening		a gap or space
opera		a play where the actors sing instead of speaking
opinion		what you think or believe
opposite		facing; on the other side
orange	*1*	a colour
	2	a round, juicy fruit
orbit		the path that a satellite or planet takes around another body in space
orchard		a field of fruit trees
orchestra		a large group of musicians who play together
orchid		a beautiful flower
order	*1*	to say what must be done
	2	tidiness
	3	the way one thing follows another
ordinary		usual; what we expect
ore		rock or earth containing metal
organ	*1*	a musical instrument
	2	a part of the body
ornament		a decoration for a person or a room
orphan		a child whose parents are dead
ostrich		the largest bird with beautiful feathers but cannot fly
other		different; not the same
otter		a water animal that has shiny brown fur and eats fish
our		belonging to us
out	*1*	not in
	2	not burning
outback		the areas of Australia far from towns
outdoors		in the open air
oval		having the shape of an egg
oven		a closed space where food is cooked by heating
over	*1*	above
	2	done; finished
overalls		a special garment worn over clothes to keep them clean
overboard		over the side of a ship
overflow		to spill over
overhead		high above; over you

Oo

owl

oyster

overseas	across the sea; abroad
overtake	to pass and leave behind
owe	to be in debt; to have to pay
owl	a bird with a large head, big eyes and a hooked beak
own	to have; to possess
ox	an animal like a cow
oxygen	one of the gases in air needed to breathe
oyster	a round and flat shellfish

Pp

paddle 1

paddle 2

palm 1

palm 2

panda

pace	1 a stride or step 2 the speed of moving
pack	1 to put into a box, case or bag 2 a group of things; a **pack** of wolves 3 to crowd into a room or other place
pad	1 a number of sheets of paper glued together on one edge 2 to walk softly 3 soft material such as cotton wool
paddle	1 a short oar used to move a canoe 2 to walk in shallow water
page	one side of a sheet of paper in a book
pageant	a parade or play in costume
pain	hurt; ache; suffering
paint	a coloured liquid to be brushed onto a surface
pair	two things of a kind that go together
pal	a close friend
palace	a large house for a king, queen or bishop
pale	weak in colour
palm	1 the inside of your hand 2 a tree with large fan-like leaves, growing in hot lands
pamphlet	a thin booklet with a paper cover
pan	a dish for cooking, usually made of metal
pancake	a thin, flat cake fried in a pan
panda	a black and white animal like a small bear that lives in and around China
panda-car	a small police car
pane	a sheet of glass in a window frame
panic	sudden fear that makes people behave in a stupid way

pansy

parachute

ırka

parrot

parsley

partridge

pansy a small, garden flower with brightly coloured petals

pant to breathe quickly as though short of breath

panther a fierce wild animal like a leopard, usually black in colour

pantomime a musical play often about a fairy story, usually seen at Christmas time

pantry a cupboard or small room with shelves where food is kept

paper material used for writing and printing on, and wrapping up things

parachute a large piece of strong cloth shaped like an umbrella, used when jumping from an aircraft

parade a march for some special event

paraffin an oil used in heaters and lamps

parallel at the same distance apart
(Railway lines are **parallel.**)

parcel something wrapped in paper and fastened

pardon to forgive; to excuse

parent father or mother

park
1 a piece of land often having grass, flowers, trees and play area
2 a place where cars may be left

parka a warm fur or cloth jacket with a hood

parliament the meeting place of the people chosen to make the laws of a country

parrot a brightly coloured bird which can be taught to say words

parsley a herb used in cooking to flavour foods

part
1 a piece; a share
2 to split up; to separate

partridge a bird with grey, white and brown feathers

party a group of people having fun

pass
1 to overtake
2 to get through a test
3 a gap between two mountains
4 to hand something to someone

passage a narrow way through; a corridor

passenger a person taken by car, train, aircraft or ship

passport a special book needed when you travel from one country to another

past time gone by

Pp

patio

pawn

pea

peach

peacock

peanut

pear

pearl

paste a thick mixture used for sticking things together

pasteurise to heat milk enough to kill germs

pastry a mixture of flour, fat and water used to make a pie or tart

pasture grassland for animals to feed on

pat to touch gently with the hand

patch material used to cover a hole

path a narrow track for walking along

patient
1 someone who is being treated by a doctor or dentist
2 able to wait without complaining

patio a paved area next to a house

pattern
1 a plan to follow such as a knitting **pattern**
2 a drawing often on curtains, wallpaper etc

pause a short break

pavement the place where we walk at the side of the road

paw an animal's foot with claws or nails

pawn one of the sixteen pieces of the lowest value in chess

pay
1 the money received for work done; wages
2 to give money for something

pea a small, round seed that grows in a pod

peace
1 a time that is calm and quiet
2 a time when there is no war

peach a round, juicy fruit with a large stone in the centre

peacock a large, male bird with a large tail which opens like a fan

peak
1 the front part of a cap
2 the top of a mountain or hill

peal the loud sound made by thunder or bells

peanut a hard, oily nut that ripens under the ground

pear a juicy fruit shaped like a cone

pearl a precious gem found inside some oyster shells

pebble a small, smooth stone often found on the beach

peck to bite or jab at food and pick it up with the beak

peculiar strange; unusual; odd

pedal the part of a machine worked by the foot such as a bicycle **pedal,** a brake **pedal** etc

pedestrian someone who walks

peel
1 the outer skin of fruit or vegetables
2 to take off the skin or outer covering

pelican

penguin

peninsula

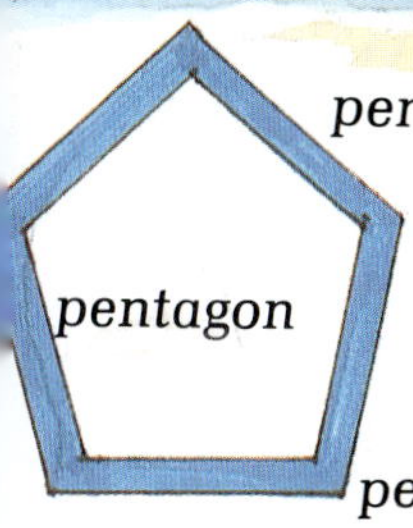

pentagon

perch 1

perch 2

periscope

peep to take a quick look

peg a small clip for holding washing on a line

pelican a large bird that has a big pouch under its long beak

pelican crossing a road crossing where the walker can control the traffic lights

pelt
1 the skin of an animal
2 to throw

pen
1 a tool used for writing
2 an enclosed space to keep animals together

pencil a writing tool made of wood with a black or coloured centre

penguin a black and white sea bird that cannot fly, found in the Antarctic

peninsula a piece of land that sticks far out into the sea

penknife a small knife with a blade that folds into the handle

penny a coin

pentagon a shape with five equal sides

people persons; men, women, boys and girls

pepper
1 a hot-tasting powder that adds flavour to food
2 a red or green vegetable often used in salads

peppermint a plant with a strong scent whose leaves are used to flavour sweets, toothpastes etc

perch
1 a freshwater fish
2 a resting place for a bird

perfect without anything wrong

perform to do something in front of an audience; to act

perfume a liquid with a pleasing smell; scent

perhaps maybe; possibly

periscope an instrument with mirrors that enables us to see from underwater, around corners or above people's heads

perish to die; to rot

permanent always there; long lasting

permit
1 to allow;
2 a ticket allowing you to do something (Simon has a **permit** to fish in the river.)

person a man, woman or child

pet an animal that you keep and take care of

petal one of the brightly coloured parts of a flower

petrol the liquid used to drive the engine of a car

petrol station a place where petrol is sold

Pp

pheasant

pier

pigeon

pigtail

pike

pincers

pheasant a wild bird with a long tail and brightly coloured feathers

phone a short way of writing 'telephone'

photograph a picture taken with a camera

pianist someone who plays the piano

piano a large musical instrument played by pressing the keys

pick
1 to gather
2 to choose
3 a pointed metal tool for breaking up hard ground

pickle food such as onions, beetroot kept in vinegar

pickpocket a thief who steals from people's pockets

picnic a meal in the open air

picture a painting, a drawing or a photograph

pie fruit or meat baked in pastry

piece a bit or part of something

pier a long platform built out over water

pierce to make a hole in something with a pointed tool

pig a farm animal kept for its meat

pigeon a bird often found in towns; some are kept as pets and trained to fly in races

piglet a young pig

pigtail hair worn like a tail

pike a fierce, freshwater fish with sharp teeth

pile a large heap

pilgrim a person who travels to a holy place

pill a little tablet or ball of medicine to be swallowed

pillar a large, strong post that supports part of a building

pillar-box a box where you post letters

pillow a cushion used on a bed

pilot
1 the person who flies an aircraft
2 the person who steers a boat into port

pimple a small lump on the skin

pin a sharp metal fastener

pinafore a kind of apron to keep clothes clean

pincers a tool for gripping

pinch to nip tightly with the fingers

pincushion a small cushion to stick pins and needles in

pineapple

pistol

pizza

plaice

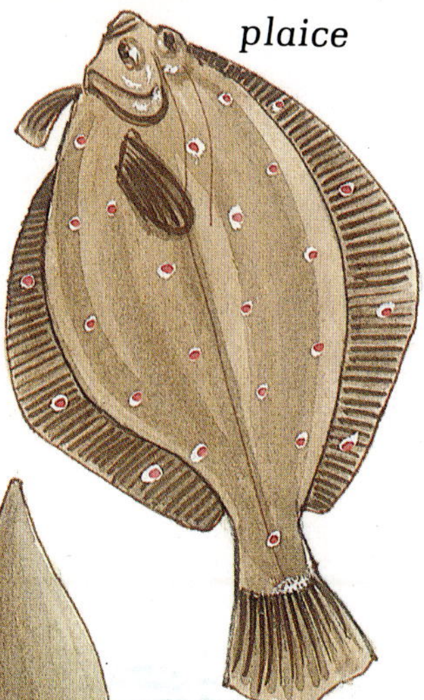

platypus

pine
1 a tall, evergreen tree with cones, and leaves that look like green needles
2 to long very much for someone or something

pineapple a large, sweet fruit that grows in hot places

pink a pale red colour

pint a measure of liquid equal to about 0.5 litre

pipe
1 a tube to carry gas or liquid
2 a tube with a bowl for smoking tobacco
3 a musical instrument

pirate a person who robs at sea

pistol a small gun fired from one hand

pit a hole in or under the ground

pitch
1 an area for playing games
2 to throw; to toss
3 tar used for road-making
4 to put up a tent

pity when we feel sorry for somebody

pizza a flat dough or pastry baked with a mixture of cheese, tomatoes, meat etc until it is crusty

place a position; a particular spot

plague a very dangerous disease that spreads quickly

plaice a flat sea fish

plain
1 easy to see or understand
2 simple; not fancy
3 a large area of flat land without trees

plan
1 a drawing of something
2 to make arrangements

plane
1 a short way of writing 'aeroplane'
2 a tool for smoothing wood

planet one of the heavenly bodies that travels round the sun

plank a thick, flat piece of wood

plant
1 any living thing that is not animal
2 to put in the ground to grow such as seeds, bulbs etc

plaster
1 a mixture used to cover walls
2 a piece of material to cover a wound

plastic a useful man-made material

plasticine a soft, clay-like material used for modelling

plate a flat dish from which we eat food

platform a raised surface such as in a hall or at a railway station

platypus a small, furry Australian mammal that has webbed feet, a beak like a duck's and lays eggs

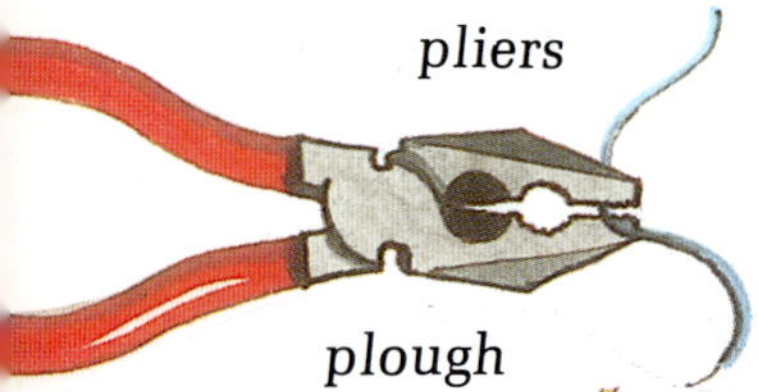
pliers

plough

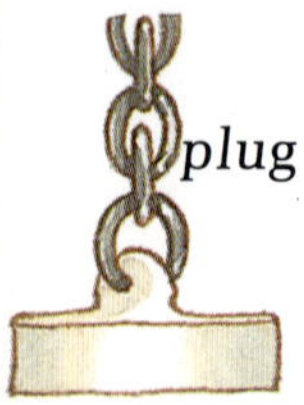
plug 1

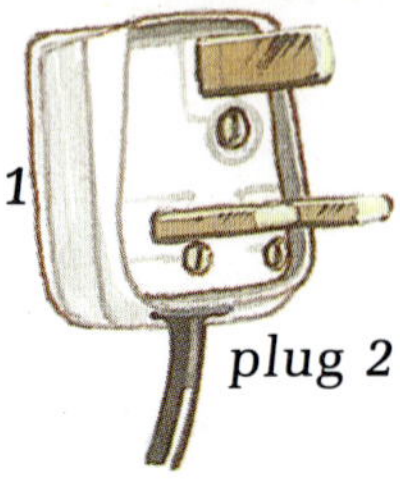
plug 2

plum

plywood

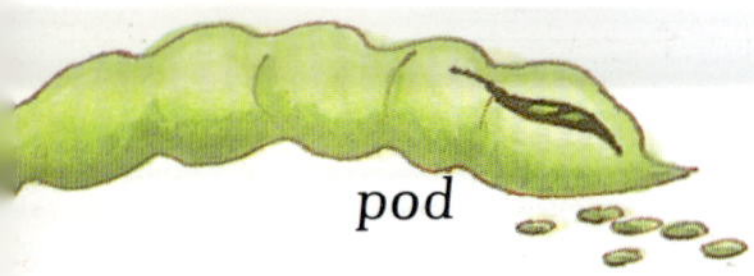
pod

polar bear

play
1 a story which is acted
2 to have fun; not to work
3 to make sounds on a musical instrument
4 to take part in a game

playground a special place for playing such as at school or in a park

playtime the time for play instead of work

pleasant enjoyable; friendly; pleasing

please
1 to make somebody happy
2 a polite word when you ask for something

plenty more than enough

pliers a tool for gripping things

plimsolls rubber soled shoes worn when playing games

plot
1 a small piece of ground
2 a secret plan
3 the story of a play

plough a machine used for turning over the soil

plug
1 a stopper for a sink or a bath
2 a piece of electrical equipment that fits into a socket

plum a soft, juicy fruit with a stone

plumber someone who fits and repairs water pipes, taps etc

plump round and fat

plunge to dive in

plural more than one

plus added to; the sign +

plywood a strong wood made by gluing together thin layers of wood

poach
1 to cook gently in water
2 to hunt or fish on someone's land without permission

pocket a small bag sewn into some clothes, for keeping things in

pod a long part of some plants with seeds inside

poem words written in verses; its lines have a rhythm and often rhyme

point
1 the sharp end
2 to show using a finger
3 a dot

poison a substance that could kill or make us very ill

poke a jab or light punch

polar having to do with the North or South Poles

polar bear a large white bear that lives in the arctic

pole a long, round piece of wood or metal

poodle

poplar

poppy

porthole

portrait

police the men and women whose job is to keep law and order

police officer a member of the police force

polish to make something smooth and bright by rubbing it

polite well behaved; well mannered

pollen a yellowish powder in the centre of flowers

pollute to make the air, land or water dirty and sometimes dangerous

polythene thin plastic made into bags and sheets

pond a small lake

pony a small horse

poodle a pet dog with very curly hair

pool a small pond

poor
1 having little money or goods
2 not very good

poorly not well

pop
1 a small bang
2 a fizzy, soft drink

poplar a tree with soft wood, that grows very quickly

poppy a flower with brightly coloured petals, usually red

popular liked by a lot of people

porch a covered entrance to a building

pork meat from a pig

porpoise an intelligent sea animal that looks like a small whale; related to a dolphin

porridge a breakfast food made by boiling oats in water

port
1 a place where ships load and unload their cargo
2 a strong wine, usually red
3 the left side of a ship or aeroplane

portable light enough to be carried

porter a person who carries luggage at an airport, station or hotel

porthole a small, round window in the side of a ship

portion a part or share

portrait a drawing, a painting or a photograph of a person

possess to have; to own

possible able to be done; likely to take place

post
1 mail; letters and parcels
2 a pole fixed in the ground

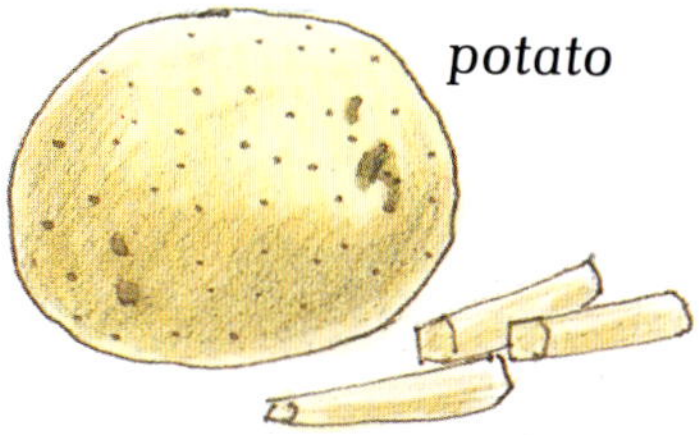
potato

poultry

prairie

prawn
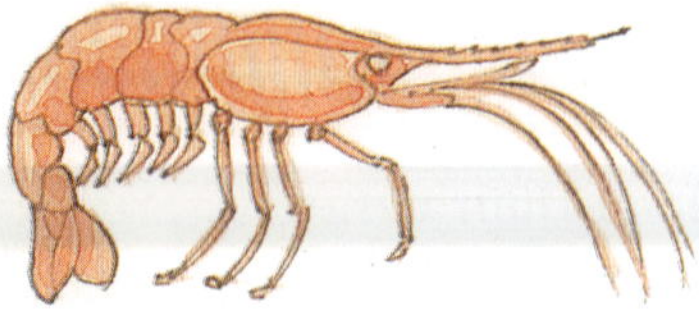

precipice

postage the charge for sending a letter or package by mail

postal code letters of the alphabet and numbers that are written after the address on any piece of mail

postcard an oblong piece of card on which a message is written, and sent through the post

poster a large printed sheet or picture put up for everyone to see and read

postman a person who delivers and collects the post

post office a building where stamps, licences, savings certificates etc can be bought and parcels can be posted

postpone to put off until another time

potato a vegetable that can be boiled, baked or fried

pottery articles such as cups and plates that are made of baked clay

pouch a small bag for carrying things

poultry farm birds such as hens, ducks and turkeys

pounce to swoop down; to leap on

pound
1 an amount of money equal to 100 pence
2 a measure of weight equal to about 0.5 kg
3 to hit very hard many times

pour
1 to make liquid run out steadily
2 to rain heavily

powder material turned into dust by pounding or grinding it

powerful very strong

practice
1 something done many times to get skill
2 all a doctor's patients

practise to do something again and again

prairie a great area of level or rolling land with grass, but few or no trees, found in Canada and USA

praise to speak highly of someone or something

pram a small carriage for a baby

prank a trick played on someone

prawn a shellfish like a large shrimp

pray to speak to God

precious very valuable

precipice a very steep, high cliff

prefer to like one thing more than another

pregnant having a baby developing inside the body

prehistoric the time before early history was written down

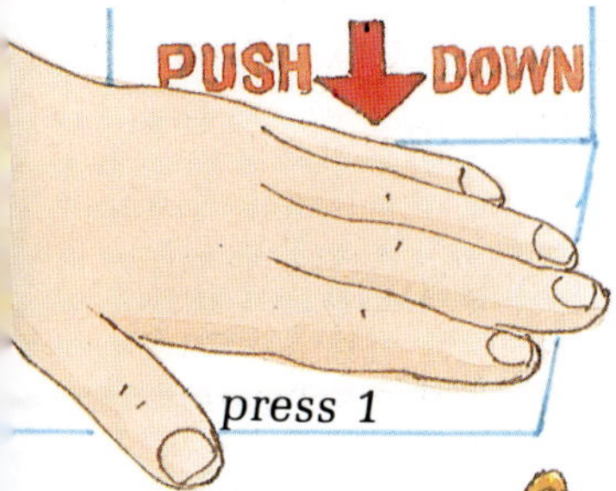

press 1

press 2

press 3

primrose

programme

prepare		to get ready
prescription		a doctor's order for medicine taken to a chemist
present	*1*	a gift to someone
	2	the time now; not the past
president		the head of a country or group (George Washington was the first **president** of the USA.)
press	*1*	to push hard
	2	a machine for printing
	3	to flatten clothes with a hot iron
pretend		to make believe
pretty		nice-looking; attractive; delighful to look at
prevent		to stop something from taking place
prey		an animal hunted by another
price		the cost of something
prick		to stab with something pointed
priest		a minister in certain Christian churches
primary		first in time or importance
prime minister		the chief minister of the government in Britain and many other countries
primrose		a yellow, wild flower that grows in Spring
prince		the son of a king or queen
princess		the daughter of a king or queen
print	*1*	to write using separate letters
	2	to press letters on to paper using a machine called a press
prison		a place where criminals are kept
private		not public; not to be shared with others
prize		a reward for doing well or winning a contest
probably		very likely
problem		a puzzle or question that is difficult to answer
produce	*1*	to make
	2	to bring out; to show
product		something that is made
profit		the money you make by selling something for more than you paid
programme		a list which tells us what is going to happen at a concert, play, game, etc
promise		words saying that you are sure to do something
prompt		done at once; quick

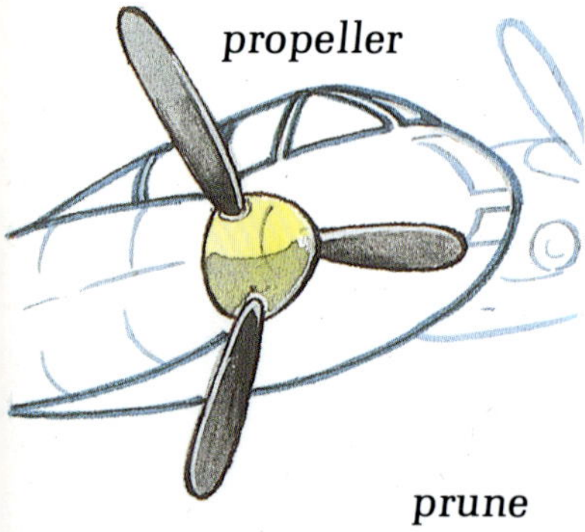
propeller

prune

puffin

puppet

pyramid

python

prop to hold up something to prevent it from falling

propeller blades that turn to drive a ship or an aircraft

properly in the correct way

property anything a person owns, especially a building or land

protect to defend from harm

proud pleased at having done well

proverb an old, wise saying

provide to supply what is needed

prune a dried plum

psalm a song from The Old Testament

public open to or belonging to everyone

pudding a soft, sweet food usually eaten after the main course

puddle a small pool of water

puffin a sea bird with a short, thick beak

pull to draw towards you

pullover a jumper pulled over the head

pulse the beating of the heart

pump a machine for forcing air or liquid along a pipe

punch to hit with the fist

puncture *1* to make a small hole in something
2 a small hole in a bicycle or car tyre

punish to make someone suffer for doing something wrong

pupil *1* someone who is being taught at school
2 the dark, centre part of the eye

puppet a doll made to move either by pulling strings or by moving the fingers

puppy a young dog

purple a colour made by mixing red and blue

purr the sound a happy cat makes

purse a small bag used for holding money

push to press against something to try to move it

pushchair a chair on wheels for young children

put to place in position

puzzle something to solve; a problem

pyjamas a set of clothes to sleep in

pyramid a building or shape which is square at the bottom and pointed at the top

python a large snake that kills its prey by squeezing it

quarry

quay

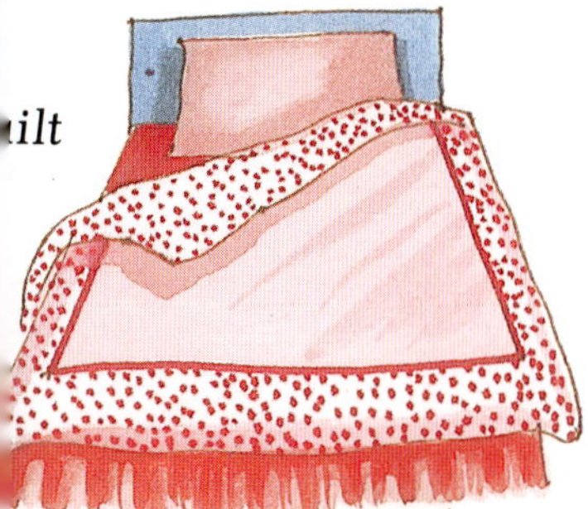
ilt

quiver 1

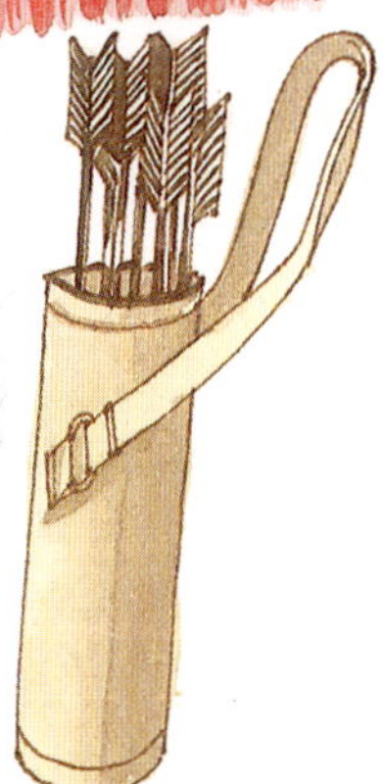
quiver 2

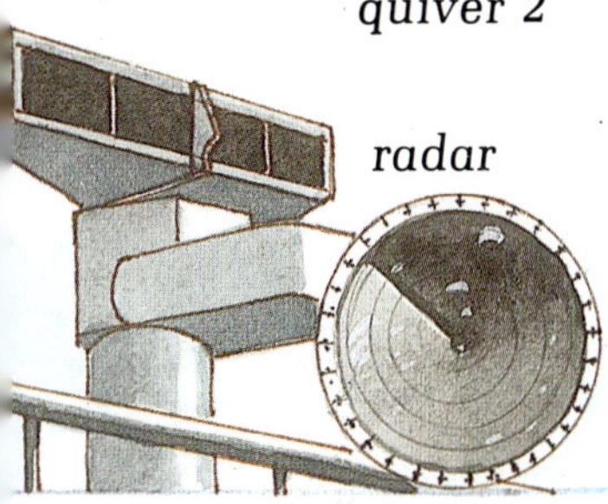
radar

Qq

quack the noise made by a duck

quaint old-fashioned in an attractive way

quake to shake; to tremble

quality how good or bad a thing is

quantity the amount of something

quarrel to disagree and argue, often using angry words

quarry a place where stone is dug from the earth

quarter one of four equal parts

quay a place where ships load and unload

queen
1 a woman who is ruler of a country or a king's wife
2 a piece in the game of chess
3 a female bee that lays eggs

queer peculiar; strange

question something asked and needing an answer

queue a line of waiting people or vehicles

quick fast; speedy

quicksand loose, wet sand into which you can sink

quiet with little or no noise; peaceful

quilt a warm covering for the bed

quite
1 completely; fully
(The story is **quite** finished.)
2 rather
(It is **quite** cold today.)

quiver
1 to tremble or shiver
2 a holder for arrows

quiz a competition in which questions have to be answered

quoits a game played with rings thrown onto a peg

Rr

rabbit a small, furry animal with long ears

race
1 a contest to see who can travel the fastest
2 a people of the same kind

rack a frame for holding things

racket
1 a loud noise
2 a bat used in games such as tennis, squash etc.

radar a method of helping to guide ships and aircraft by using radio waves

radiator
1 a heating device used for warming a room
2 the part of the car that keeps the engine cool

radio
1 a way of sending and receiving sounds by electrical waves
2 an instrument for receiving these waves

radish a small, red-skinned vegetable used in salads

raft logs or planks tied together to make a kind of boat

rag a piece of waste cloth, often used for cleaning

rage great anger

ragged untidy; badly torn

raid a sudden, unexpected attack

rail a metal or wooden bar

railing a fence made of rails

railway
1 a track for trains
2 tracks, station, trains, and everything to do with them

rain drops of water falling from the clouds

rainbow an arch of seven colours seen in the sky when the sun shines through light rain

raincoat a waterproof coat

raise to lift up; to bring up

raisin a small dried grape

rake a garden tool fitted with spikes

ram
1 a male sheep
2 to crash into

ramble
1 a country walk
2 to talk in a way that confuses people

ranch a large farm on which cattle, horses or sheep are raised

range
1 a line of mountains or hills
2 the distance a weapon can shoot

ranger a person who looks after a forest, a large park or a game reserve

rap a quick, sharp tap

rapid very fast

rapids a part of a river where the water moves very fast, often over rocks

rare scarce; not often seen

rash
1 small spots that appear on your skin
2 doing something without thinking

raspberry a small, red, juicy fruit with many seeds

rat an animal like a large mouse

rattlesnake

raven

ravine

rectangle

reel 1

el 2

reel 3

rattle	1	the sound made by shaking a lot of hard things together
	2	a baby's toy that makes this sound
rattlesnake		a poisonous snake that makes a rattling sound with its tail
rave		to shout and scream; to talk excitedly
raven		a large, shiny, black bird
ravine		a deep, narrow valley
raw	1	not cooked
	2	very cold
ray		a thin beam of light
razor		an instrument used for shaving
reach	1	to stretch out and touch or get
	2	to arrive at
read		to look at words and understand their meaning
ready		prepared
real		true, not imaginary
realize		to understand clearly
reason		why a thing is done or said
rebel		to rise against the leader
rebound		to bounce back
receipt		a paper saying that you have paid for something
receive		to take; to accept what is given to you
recipe		directions on how to cook food
recognize		to know something or somebody
record	1	a flat disc to be played on a record player
	2	the best performance
	3	a written account or diary
recorder		a wind instrument made of wood or plastic
record-player		a machine for playing records
recover	1	to get better after an illness
	2	to get something back
rectangle		a four sided shape that has four straight sides and four square corners
red		a colour; the colour of blood
reed		a tall grass that grows at the edge of water
reef		rocks just below the surface of the sea
reel	1	a Scottish dance
	2	something to wind thread or film onto
	3	to stagger about
referee		a person who makes sure that a game is played fairly

settee

shadow

shaggy

shamrock

shark

shears

serve
1 to work for someone
2 to give out food to others
3 to sell things in a store
4 to play the first shot in table tennis, badminton etc.

set
1 a group of things that go together such as a **set** of golf clubs
2 to put things in place
(Please **set** the table for lunch.)
3 a television or radio receiver
4 to become solid

settee a long seat for more than one person

settle
1 to agree upon
2 to go to live somewhere

several more than two or three, but not many

sew to stitch with a needle and thread

sewer an underground drain pipe that carries away waste from houses and other buildings

shabby old and ragged; almost worn out

shade
1 a place hidden from the sun
2 a cover for a light

shadow the dark shape caused by something standing in the way of a light

shaggy having long, thick, rough hair

shake
1 to move something quickly from side to side or up and down
2 to shiver; to tremble

shallow not deep

shame a feeling of being unhappy or foolish because you have done wrong

shampoo a liquid soap for washing hair

shamrock a plant with bright green leaves that are in three parts

shape the outline or form of anything

share
1 the part given to each person
2 to divide out

shark a large, fierce sea fish that has many sharp teeth

sharp
1 with an edge or point that can easily make a cut
2 sudden
(We came to a **sharp** bend in the road.)
3 quick to understand or notice; intelligent

shave to cut off hair using a razor

shear to cut the wool off a sheep

shears large scissors used for cutting hedges, grass, wool etc

rattlesnake

raven

ravine

rectangle

reel 1

reel 2

reel 3

rattle	*1* the sound made by shaking a lot of hard things together *2* a baby's toy that makes this sound
rattlesnake	a poisonous snake that makes a rattling sound with its tail
rave	to shout and scream; to talk excitedly
raven	a large, shiny, black bird
ravine	a deep, narrow valley
raw	*1* not cooked *2* very cold
ray	a thin beam of light
razor	an instrument used for shaving
reach	*1* to stretch out and touch or get *2* to arrive at
read	to look at words and understand their meaning
ready	prepared
real	true, not imaginary
realize	to understand clearly
reason	why a thing is done or said
rebel	to rise against the leader
rebound	to bounce back
receipt	a paper saying that you have paid for something
receive	to take; to accept what is given to you
recipe	directions on how to cook food
recognize	to know something or somebody
record	*1* a flat disc to be played on a record player *2* the best performance *3* a written account or diary
recorder	a wind instrument made of wood or plastic
record-player	a machine for playing records
recover	*1* to get better after an illness *2* to get something back
rectangle	a four sided shape that has four straight sides and four square corners
red	a colour; the colour of blood
reed	a tall grass that grows at the edge of water
reef	rocks just below the surface of the sea
reel	*1* a Scottish dance *2* something to wind thread or film onto *3* to stagger about
referee	a person who makes sure that a game is played fairly

refrigerator

reindeer

reins

reptile

rescue

reflect		to throw back light, heat or sound
refreshments		something to eat or drink
refrigerator		a fridge; a container that keeps things cold
refugee		someone who has fled from one place to another to find safety
refuse		to say no; to decline
register		a written list of names
regret		to be very sorry about
rehearse		to practise, such as a play, in order to be ready for a performance
reign		the period a king or queen reigns
reindeer		a large deer that has antlers and lives in the cold, northern lands
reins		the straps used to control and guide a horse
rejoice		to show how pleased or happy you are
relative		a person who belongs to the same family as someone else
relax		to take a rest and enjoy yourself
release		to let go
remain		to stay behind
remember		to bring back to mind; to recall
Remembrance Day		November 11, the day we honour the people who died in the First and Second World Wars
remind		to help someone remember
remove	*1*	to take away
	2	to move from one place to another
rent		money paid for the use of a flat, car, video-recorder etc that you do not own
repair		to mend; to put right
repeat		to say or do something again
replace	*1*	to put back in its place
	2	to take the place of
reply		to answer
report		to tell about something that has happened
reporter		someone who collects news for a newspaper, radio and television
reptile		a cold blooded animal with a body covered in scaly skin
require		to need
rescue		to save from danger or harm

reservoir

rhinoceros

rhubarb

rifle

ring-road

reservoir	a place where water is collected and stored for later use
rest	*1* the others; what is left *2* to be still; to stop working
restaurant	a place where you buy and eat a meal
result	something that happens because of something else
retire	to give up work, usually because of age
retreat	to go back
return	*1* to come back to a place *2* to give back
reverse	*1* to go backwards *2* to turn something the other way
revolver	a hand gun that can fire several times before it has to be reloaded
reward	money or a prize given for something done
rhinoceros	a large, thick-skinned African animal with one or two horns on its nose
rhubarb	a garden plant whose stalks can be cooked and eaten
rhyme	word endings that sound alike
rhythm	the steady beat or time of music or poetry
rib	one of the bones of your chest
ribbon	a narrow band of material
rice	a food grain that grows in warm, wet parts of the world
rich	having much money; wealthy
ride	to travel in a vehicle or on an animal's back
rifle	a long gun that is fired from the shoulder
right	*1* the opposite of left *2* what is good; the opposite of wrong
rim	the outer edge of a cup, wheel, bowl etc
ring	*1* a round piece of metal, usually gold, to wear on a finger *2* a circle *3* the sound of a bell
ring-road	a road built to go round a busy town
rink	a sheet of ice used by skaters and ice-hockey players
rinse	to use clean water to wash away soap or dirt
riot	a violent and noisy disturbance caused by a crowd of people
rip	a tear; a split
ripe	ready to be picked and eaten
rise	*1* to get up *2* to go higher

robin

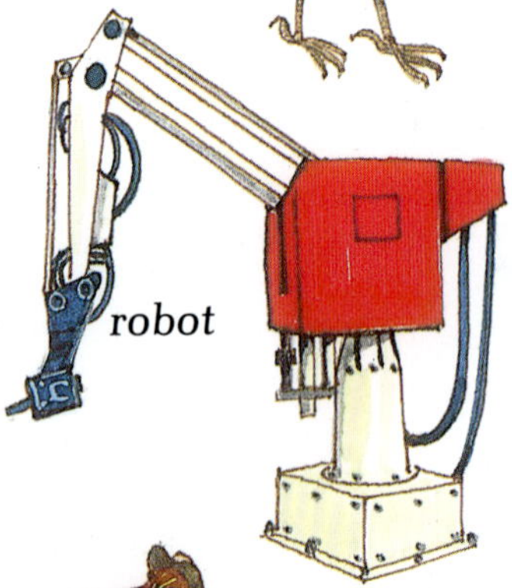

robot

rodeo

roller-coaster

risk	a chance, sometimes dangerous
river	a large stream
road	a hard, wide track on which vehicles travel
roam	to wander about
roar	a loud deep sound made by a lion, thunder, heavy traffic, waterfall etc
roast	to cook by dry heat in an oven
rob	to steal
robin	a small garden bird with a red breast
robot	a machine that can do some work done by humans
rock	*1* a large piece of stone *2* to move gently back and forth *3* a sweet, often mint-flavoured, in a long stick *4* a kind of pop music
rocket	*1* a firework at the end of stick that goes high in the air when lit *2* a device for sending up spacecraft
rod	a long thin stiff stick of wood or metal
rodent	any of a group of animals that have sharp front teeth used in gnawing
rodeo	a contest of skill in riding horses, roping cattle etc
rogue	a very dishonest person; a cheat
roll	*1* to turn over and over *2* a small round piece of bread *3* something the shape of a tube *4* the sound made by drums
roller	*1* a heavy cylinder rolled to make things flat *2* a kind of hair curler *3* a large, long wave in the sea
roller coaster	a thrilling railway ride at an amusement park
roller skate	a skate that has four small wheels on the bottom
roof	the outside covering of a building or a vehicle
rook	a large, black bird of the crow family
room	*1* a part of a building *2* space to put things
root	the part of the plant that grows in the soil
rope	a thick cord
rose	a garden flower with a thorny stem, growing on a bush
rosy	pink in colour
rot	to go bad; to decay

roundabout 1

roundabout 2

ruby

rucksack

rudder

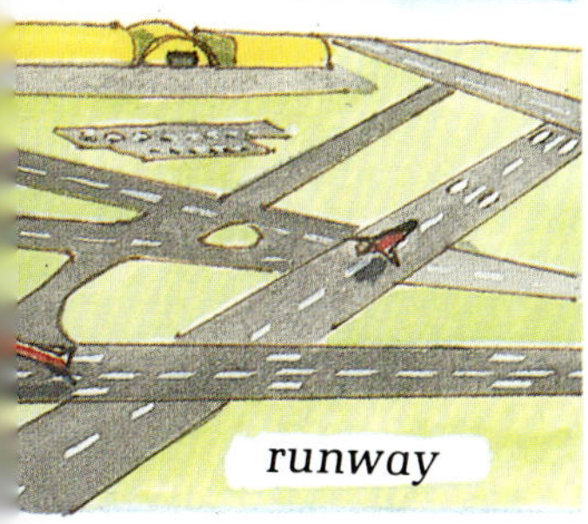

runway

rotate to turn round in circles

rotten gone bad; spoiled; decayed

rough
1 not smooth; uneven
2 stormy

round
1 in the shape of a circle
2 a period in a boxing match

roundabout
1 a traffic island in the centre of busy crossroads
2 a ride at a fair

rounders a game played by two sides with bat and ball

route a way of getting to a place

row (as in now) a loud noise; a quarrel

row (as in low)
1 to make a boat move by using oars
2 a line of people or things

rowing-boat a small boat that is moved with oars

royal having to do with kings or queens or their families

rub to move one thing against another many times

rubber
1 material made from the sap of a rubber tree used to make tyres, elastic bands etc
2 a piece of this material used for removing pencil marks

rubbish
1 waste things that are of no use
2 nonsense

ruby a deep red precious stone

rucksack a bag-fastened to the shoulders, in which walkers and climbers can carry their belongings

rudder the part used to steer a boat or an aircraft

rude bad mannered; not polite

rug
1 a small carpet
2 a kind of blanket

rugby a game played with an oval ball

ruin
1 what is left of an old building
2 to spoil; to wreck

rule
1 a law we must follow
2 to govern

ruler
1 a person who rules a country
2 a strip of marked material, used for drawing straight lines and for measuring

rumble a deep, rolling sound

run to move quickly on your feet

rung one of the steps of a ladder

runway where an aircraft lands and takes off

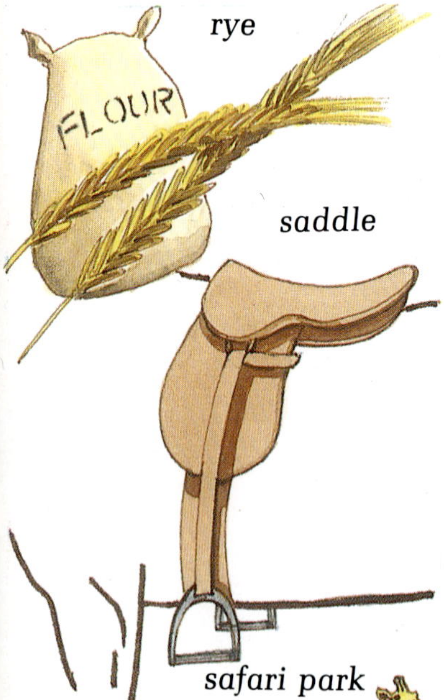
rye

saddle

safari park

salmon

sampan

sand dune

rush to hurry; to move quickly

rust a reddish-brown coating that forms on metal

rustle a soft, crackling sound like the **rustle** of leaves in the wind

rut a groove left by a wheel in soft ground

rye a grain used for making flour and as food for animals

Ss

sack a large bag made of strong material

sad not happy

saddle a seat for a rider of a horse

safari a journey to see or hunt wild animals

safari park a large area of land where wild animals are collected together so that they can be seen by people in vehicles

safe
1 a strong, steel box for keeping money and valuables
2 out of danger

sag to bend downwards in the middle

sail
1 a sheet of strong cloth that is attached to a boat to drive it along
2 to travel over the water

sailor a member of a ship's crew

saint a man or woman who has lived a very holy life

salad a mixture of vegetables and fruit eaten cold

sale
1 when things are sold
2 the time when shops sell goods cheaper than usual

salmon a large fish with pink flesh, used for food

salt a white powder used for flavouring food

same not different; exactly alike

sampan a Chinese flat-bottomed boat

sample a small piece of something that shows you what the rest is like

sand tiny grains of rock and shells

sandals open shoes fastened with straps

sand dune a mound of sand on a desert or by the sea

sandwich two slices of bread with meat or other food as a filling

sap the liquid inside plants and trees

sardine a small, silvery fish sold for food, usually sold in tins

sari

phone

scaffolding

scarecrow

sari a piece of clothing worn by women and girls in India and other Asian countries

satchel a child's school bag

satellite
1 a heavenly body that travels round a planet
2 a man-made object moving in orbit around the earth

satisfy to make someone pleased

sauce a liquid for flavouring food

saucepan a cooking pot with a lid and long handle

saucer a round dish for a cup to stand on

sausage chopped meat and spices stuffed into a skin

savage wild and fierce

save
1 to bring out of danger
2 to keep something to use it later on

savings money that has been saved

saw a metal cutting-tool with sharp, pointed teeth

saxophone a musical instrument, played by blowing and pushing down the keys

say to speak; to tell

scab a crust that forms over a wound

scaffolding platforms for builders to stand on when working high up

scald to burn from very hot liquid or steam

scale
1 a weighing machine
2 one of the many thin, hard flakes on the skin of fish or reptile
3 a set of musical notes

scalp the skin and hair on top of your head

Ss

scan to look at quickly

scar a mark left on the skin by a wound

scarce not plentiful; rare

scare to frighten

scarecrow a figure like a person dressed in old clothes set up in a field to frighten birds away from a farmer's crops

scarf a long piece of cloth worn round the neck

scarlet a very bright red colour

scatter to throw around in several directions

scene
1 a view; a picture
2 a part of a play
3 a place where something happened

schooner

scorpion

seagull

seahorse

seal 1

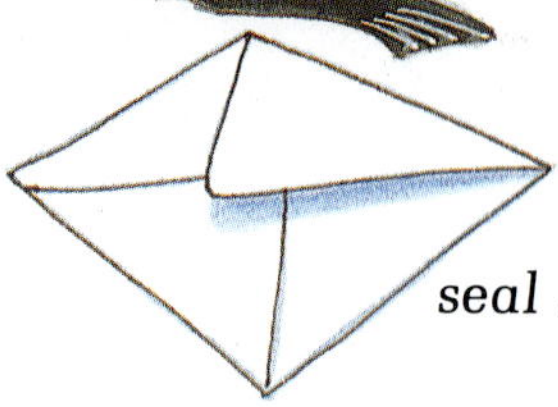
seal 2

scent	*1* a smell; a perfume *2* the trail of an animal
scholar	someone who is learning
school	*1* a place where people, usually children, are taught *2* a large group of fish swimming together
schooner	a large sailing ship that has two or more masts on it
science	knowledge got from making experiments and careful study
scissors	a cutting tool with two blades fastened together
scooter	a small, two-wheeled toy for riding; a type of cycle driven by a petrol engine
scorch	to burn slightly
score	*1* the number of goals, runs, tries etc in a game *2* to make a goal or a run in a game
scorpion	a stinging insect with a long tail
scout	*1* a member of the Boy Scouts *2* someone sent ahead to gather information
scramble	*1* to climb or crawl using hands and feet *2* to mix together
scrap	*1* a small piece *2* rubbish
scrape	*1* to scratch things off *2* a hard, grating sound
scratch	*1* to make a mark with something sharp *2* to rub the part of your skin where it itches
scream	a high-sounding shrill cry or shout
screen	the surface on which television pictures or films are shown
screw	a kind of nail with grooves round it that goes into wood or metal by being turned
screwdriver	a tool for turning screws
scribble	to write badly and hurriedly
scrub	to clean by rubbing hard
sculptor	someone who carves statues or shapes
sea	the vast body of salt water that covers three quarters of the earth's surface
seagull	a large, grey and white bird that lives near water
seahorse	a small sea animal with a neck and head that look like those of a horse
seal	*1* a large, furry sea animal that lives in and by the sea *2* to stick and fasten an envelope

seaside

seaweed

see-saw

sentry

sergeant

search		to look everywhere for something
seaside		land near the sea
season	*1*	the time of the year such as spring, summer, autumn or winter
	2	to add salt, pepper, or other flavours to food
seat		something to sit on
seat belt		a strong belt to hold a person in the seat of a car or aircraft in case of a bump or crash
seaweed		a green or brown plant that grows in the sea
second	*1*	the one after the first
	2	a very small measure of time. Sixty **seconds** make one minute.
second-hand		used by someone else before you
secret		something that you keep to yourself and one or two close friends
secretary		someone who prepares letters, keeps records and arranges meetings etc
section		a part
see		what you do when you use your eyes
seed		a tiny grain from a plant from which a new plant grows
seem		to appear to be (You **seem** to be very unhappy.)
see-saw		a plank on which children sit and go up and down
seldom		rarely; not often
selfish		thinking and caring only about yourself
sell		to hand over something in return for money
send		to make someone or something go somewhere
senior		someone older or more important
sense	*1*	to be able to see, hear, smell, taste or touch
	2	what makes you behave in a wise way
sentence	*1*	a group of words making complete sense and usually ending in a full stop or a question mark
	2	a punishment given in a court of law
sentry		a soldier on guard
separate		to divide one thing from another
sergeant		a rank in the army or police force
serial		a story told in parts or sections
serious	*1*	of great importance
	2	thoughtful; not joking
servant		someone who is paid to work in someone else's house

settee

shadow

shaggy

shamrock

shark

shears

serve
1 to work for someone
2 to give out food to others
3 to sell things in a store
4 to play the first shot in table tennis, badminton etc.

set
1 a group of things that go together such as a **set** of golf clubs
2 to put things in place
(Please **set** the table for lunch.)
3 a television or radio receiver
4 to become solid

settee
a long seat for more than one person

settle
1 to agree upon
2 to go to live somewhere

several
more than two or three, but not many

sew
to stitch with a needle and thread

sewer
an underground drain pipe that carries away waste from houses and other buildings

shabby
old and ragged; almost worn out

shade
1 a place hidden from the sun
2 a cover for a light

shadow
the dark shape caused by something standing in the way of a light

shaggy
having long, thick, rough hair

shake
1 to move something quickly from side to side or up and down
2 to shiver; to tremble

shallow
not deep

shame
a feeling of being unhappy or foolish because you have done wrong

shampoo
a liquid soap for washing hair

shamrock
a plant with bright green leaves that are in three parts

shape
the outline or form of anything

share
1 the part given to each person
2 to divide out

shark
a large, fierce sea fish that has many sharp teeth

sharp
1 with an edge or point that can easily make a cut
2 sudden
(We came to a **sharp** bend in the road.)
3 quick to understand or notice; intelligent

shave
to cut off hair using a razor

shear
to cut the wool off a sheep

shears
large scissors used for cutting hedges, grass, wool etc

shed a small building, usually made of wood, for storing things

sheep an animal that is raised for its wool and meat

sheet
1 a large piece of thin cloth used on a bed
2 any thin flat piece such as a **sheet** of paper or a **sheet** of glass

shelf a board fixed to a wall to hold things

shell
1 a hard covering for some land or sea animals
2 the hard covering of a nut or egg
3 a large bullet that explodes when it hits something

shelter a place where you are safe from the weather or danger

shepherd someone who looks after sheep

sheriff a person who keeps law and order in parts of U.S.A.

shield
1 a piece of armour once carried by soldiers
2 to protect or guard

shift to move something; to change your position

shin the front of your leg between the knee and the ankle

shine
1 to give out light
2 to polish

shingle small stones on a beach

ship a sea-going boat

shipwreck a ship that is damaged and sinks at sea

shirt a piece of clothing with a collar and sleeves

shiver to shake with fear or cold

shoal a large number of fish of the same kind swimming together

shock a sudden fright; an unpleasant surprise

shoe footwear worn below the ankles

shoot
1 to kick a ball at goal
2 a young growth on a plant
3 to fire a gun

shop a building where things are sold

shore land at the edge of the sea or a lake

short
1 not long in time or distance
2 not having enough

shorts very short trousers

shoulder the place where your arm joins your body

shout to raise your voice and call loudly

shove to push

shovel a wide spade

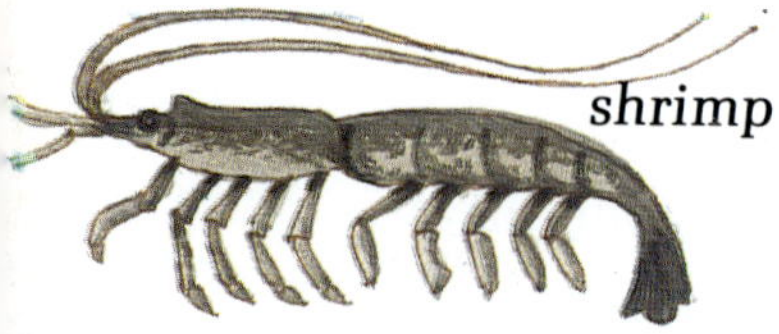

shrimp

shrub

sideboard

silk

silver

show
1 to let someone see something
2 to explain; to make clear
3 a form of entertainment such as a concert, display etc

shower
1 a gentle fall of rain
2 a spray of water to wash the body

shriek to give a very high scream

shrimp a small, grey shellfish that turns pink when cooked

shrink to become smaller

shrub a plant like a small, bushy tree

shut
1 to close
2 not open

shy afraid to speak to or meet people

sick not well; ill

side
1 a team of players
2 one face of an object

sideboard furniture in which we keep things used at meals

sigh to breathe out heavily to show that you are tired, bored or unhappy

sight
1 something that is seen
2 when we are able to see

sign
1 to write your name
2 a notice that tells something, such as a traffic **sign**
3 a movement of the body, such as nodding the head

signal a message or sign telling us what to do

signature your name written by yourself in your own way

signpost a post which has signs showing the way and distances

silent not making a sound

silk a smooth, shiny material made from threads spun by silkworms

silly foolish; stupid

silver a precious, shiny white metal

similar nearly the same

simple
1 easy
2 plain; not fancy
(Kerry wore a **simple** dress.)

sin a wrong or wicked deed

since
1 from that time until now
2 because
(**Since** it is your birthday, you may have a party.)

sincere honest and true

sing to make tunes with the voice

siren

skate

ski

skylark

sledge

singer a person who sings

single
1 not married
2 one only
3 a small record

sink
1 to go under water
2 a basin with taps and a drain

sip to drink in small amounts

siren a machine that makes a loud screaming noise as a warning

sister
1 a girl with the same parents as ourselves
2 a nurse in charge of a ward in a hospital

sit to rest on your bottom

size how big a thing is

skate a boot fitted with a metal blade, or with four small wheels

skeleton all the 206 bones of the body

ski one of two long narrow boards on which a person can stand and slide over the snow

skid a sudden slide on something slippery or very smooth

skill the ability to do something well

skin the outer covering of people, animals, and some fruit and vegetables

skin-diver a person who can swim under water for long periods of time

skip
1 to jump lightly from one leg to the other, often over a rope
2 to leave out parts

skipper a captain of a ship; a captain of a sports team

skirt a garment for girls and women that hangs from the waist

skittles wooden blocks knocked down with a ball

skull the bony part of your head

sky where the sun, moon, stars and clouds are seen

skylark a small, song-bird which flies high in the sky

skyscraper a building that is very tall

slack loose; not tight

slam to bang hard

slap to hit with the open hand

slay to kill

sledge a vehicle on runners which will move smoothly on snow

sleeve

sling

slippers

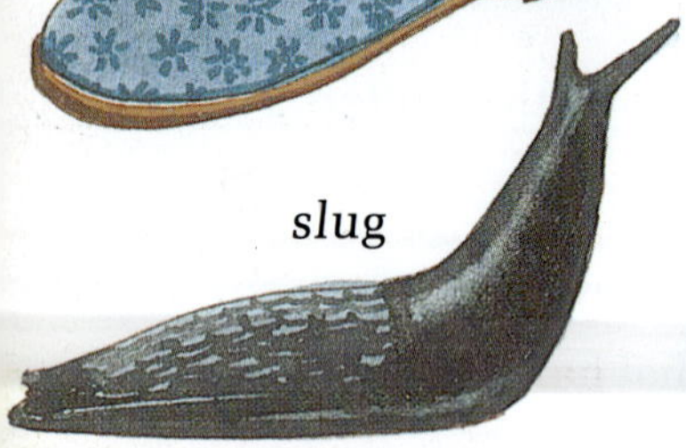

slug

snail

snake

sleep	to rest completely with closed eyes
sleet	a mixture of snow and rain
sleeve	the part of a garment that covers your arm
slice	a thin, flat piece cut from something
slide	*1* to move smoothly over a slippery surface *2* a hair-fastener
slim	not fat; tall and thin
sling	a bandage hanging from the neck, which will support an injured arm
slip	*1* to lose your balance and fall *2* a small mistake *3* a loose garment worn under a dress or skirt
slippers	soft shoes worn indoors
slope	ground that goes up or down; a slant
slow	taking a long time; not quick
slug	a kind of snail without a shell
sly	not to be trusted; crafty
smack	a hard hit with the open hand
small	little
smart	*1* neat and well dressed *2* quick to understand
smash	to break into pieces; to crash
smell	to be aware of something by using your nose
smile	a happy look on your face
smoke	*1* a dark cloud from something burning *2* to burn tobacco in a pipe or cigarette
smooth	even and flat; not rough or bumpy
smudge	a dirty mark
smuggle	to take things into the country secretly and not pay tax on them
snack	a light meal that is easy to get ready
snail	a small, slow creature with a shell on its back
snake	a long, smooth reptile without legs
snap	*1* to break suddenly with a sharp noise *2* to speak in an angry way *3* a photograph *4* to bite at angrily
snare	a trap used to catch animals
snarl	a low, growling sound

snorkel

snowdrop
snowflake

snowplough

soldier

somersault

snatch		to grab things quickly
sneak	1	to move, trying not to be seen or heard
	2	a sly, dishonest person
sneeze		a sudden, noisy rush of air from your nose
sniff		to take in little, short breaths through your nose
snip		to cut a little bit off
snore		to breathe noisily while you are asleep
snorkel		a tube allowing swimmers to breathe while swimming just below the surface
snow		frozen raindrops that fall as white flakes
snowball		a ball made of tightly packed snow
snowdrop		a tiny, white flower seen at the start of spring
snowflake		one piece of snow
snowman		snow made into the shape of a man
snowplough		a machine for clearing snow from roads
soak		to make very wet
soap		a liquid or solid material used for washing
soar		to rise high in the sky
sob		to weep noisily
soccer		football played with a round ball
sock		a short covering for the foot
sofa		a long seat like a settee
soft	1	not hard
	2	quiet; not loud
soil		ground in which plants grow
solar		having to do with the sun
soldier		someone who belongs to an army
sole	1	the bottom of the foot, or of footwear
	2	a flat fish that lives in the sea
solid		hard; not hollow
solo	1	on your own
	2	a piece of music to be played or sung by one person
solve		to find the answer to a puzzle or a mystery
some		a few; not all
somebody		a certain person
somersault		to turn over and over, head over heels
something		anything; a thing not clearly known
sometimes		now and then; once in a while

souvenir
space shuttle
spaniel
sparrow
spear

somewhere	in a place not clearly known
son	a male child
song	music made by the voice
soon	in a short time; before long
sore	*1* painful *2* a place on the body which is painful
sorry	feeling unhappy at something that has happened, or something you have done
sort	*1* a kind (What **sort** of dog do you have?) *2* to put things in groups of the same kind
sound	a noise; something that you hear
soup	a liquid food made by boiling meat, fish, or vegetables in water
sour	bitter to taste; not sweet
south	the opposite to the north
souvenir	something you keep to remind you of a certain place or time
sow (like how)	a female pig
sow (like low)	to plant seeds
space	*1* the distance between things *2* all the places beyond the earth's atmosphere
spaceship	a vehicle built to travel in space
space shuttle	a vehicle that travels to and fro between earth and a space station
spade	a garden tool used for digging
spaghetti	a food made of flour and water rolled into long, thin sticks or strings
spaniel	a dog with long hair, drooping ears, and short legs
spare	*1* left over; not being used *2* to be able to give (I can **spare** some apples, I have plenty.)
spark	a tiny, burning bit
sparkle	to glitter; to give off sparks of light
sparrow	a small bird with brown, grey and white feathers
spawn	the eggs of fish, frogs, toads, newts and other water animals
speak	to say something
spear	a sharp, pointed weapon with a long, thin handle
special	not ordinary; different from others in a certain way

spectacles

speedometer

sphere

spinach

spiral

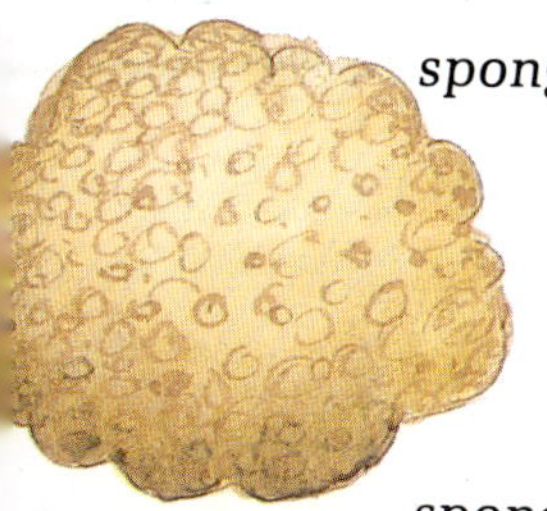

sponge 1

sponge 2

speck a tiny bit; a small spot

spectacles glasses for the eyes to help us see better

spectator someone who watches others doing something

speech
1 the sound we make when we speak
2 a talk given on a special occasion

speed how quickly something moves or happens

speedometer an instrument that shows the speed of a vehicle

spell
1 to arrange letters to make words
2 words supposed to have magic power

spend
1 to pay out money
2 to use time
(We are going to **spend** our holidays in Cornwall.)

sphere a ball shape

spice part of a plant used to flavour food

spider a small, eight-legged creature that spins a web to catch insects for food

spike a sharp point

spill to let a liquid overflow

spin
1 to turn round and round quickly
2 to make thread by twisting

spinach a dark green, leafy vegetable

spine the backbone of a person or some animals

spiral a curve that keeps winding

spire the pointed, upper part of a church tower or steeple

spit to force something out of your mouth

splash
1 the noise made when something falls into water
2 to throw water about

Ss

splendid excellent; wonderful

split
1 to break or cut from end to end
2 a crack; a long, thin break

spoil to ruin or damage something

spoke a thin rod or bar that connects the rim of a wheel to the centre

sponge
1 a soft pad, full of holes, that soaks up liquid
2 a soft cake

spoon a tool used for eating or stirring liquids and soft foods

sport games or pastimes, often played outside

spot
1 a small mark
2 to see; to notice something

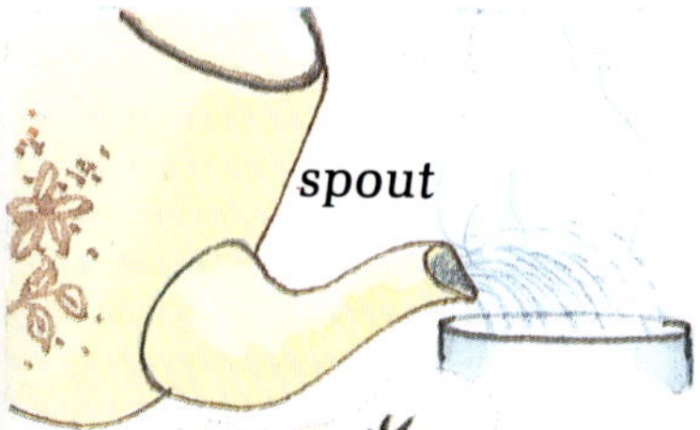
spout

springbok

spruce

squirrel

stadium

spout		the narrow part of a container through which a liquid flows
sprain		to twist a part of the body so that it becomes painful
spray	*1*	to send out tiny drops of liquid
	2	a bunch of flowers
spread	*1*	to cover a surface
	2	to stretch out
spring	*1*	the season after winter
	2	a place where water flows out of the ground
	3	a metal coil
	4	to jump up suddenly
springbok		a kind of South African antelope
sprinkle		to scatter tiny bits or drops of liquid
sprint		to run very quickly for a short distance
sprout		to begin to grow
spruce		an evergreen tree with cones, and needle-like leaves
spurt		a sudden rush of liquid
spy		someone who tries to find out secret information, usually from an enemy
square		a shape with four equal sides
squash	*1*	to crush; to squeeze tightly together
	2	a fruit drink
	3	an indoor game played with rackets and a hollow ball
squeak		a short, high sound, like that made by a mouse
squeal		a long, high call
squeeze		to press hard
squirrel		a small animal with a long fluffy tail that lives in trees
squirt		to send out a jet of water
stable		a building in which horses are kept
stack		a large pile
stadium		a sports ground with rows of seats all round
staff		a group of people who work together in a school, hospital etc
stage	*1*	a platform for acting
	2	a part of a journey
stage-coach		a large, closed coach, pulled by horses
stagger		to walk in an unsteady way
stain	*1*	a dirty mark
	2	a dye often used on wood

stalk 1
stalk 2

stampede

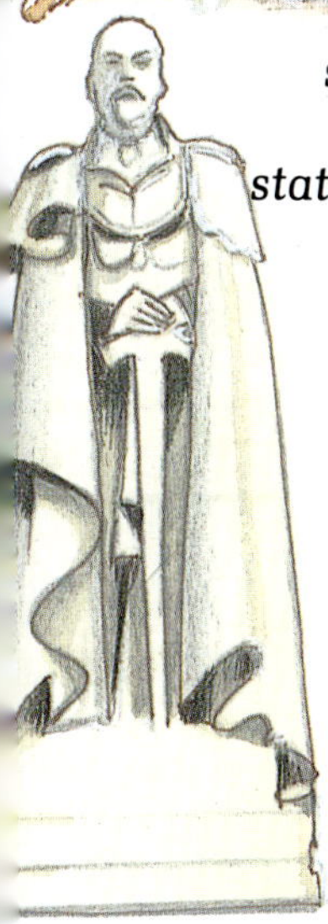
statue

steeple

stairs		a number of steps leading from one floor of a building to another
stale		old; not fresh
stalk	*1*	the stem of a flower or plant
	2	to track an animal quietly
stallion		a male horse
stamp	*1*	to bang the foot on the ground
	2	a small piece of paper, sticky on one side, to pay for postage
stampede		a sudden rush of frightened people or animals
stand	*1*	to be on your feet
	2	seats under cover at a sports ground
star	*1*	a heavenly body that looks like a speck of light at night
	2	an outstanding actor, singer, sports player etc
starboard		the right side of a ship or aeroplane
starfish		a small sea creature that has a flat body shaped like a star
starling		a common bird with dark, glossy feathers
start	*1*	to begin
	2	to make a sudden movement
starve		to be very ill or die because there is not enough food to eat
station		a place at which trains begin or stop on a journey
stationary		not moving
stationery		paper, envelopes and writing materials
statue		a figure made of stone, metal or other materials
stay		to remain behind
steady		firm; not wobbling
steak		a slice of meat or fish for cooking
steal		to take something that is not yours and keep it
steam		the white cloud or vapour, that comes from boiling water
steel		a strong metal made from iron
steep		going up or down sharply; having a sharp slope
steeple		a tall pointed church tower
steer		to guide a motor vehicle or a boat
stem		the part of the plant from which the leaves grow
step	*1*	a pace forward or backward
	2	one stair on a staircase
	3	the stone slab in front of a door
stereo		short for stereophonic sound

stickleback

stilts

stirrup

stork

stern
1 the back part of a ship
2 strict; firm

stew
meat with vegetables cooked slowly in water

steward/ stewardess
a person in charge of food and other services on an aircraft or a ship

stick
1 a short piece of wood
2 to fasten together by using glue

stickleback
a small fish with spines on its back that lives in ponds and streams

stiff
1 not easy to bend
2 difficult
(It was a **stiff** climb to the top of the cliff.)

stile
steps to help you over a fence or wall

still
quiet; not moving; peaceful

stilts
two poles, each with a step part way up, for walking high above the ground

sting
a painful stab of poison from an insect or plant

stink
a bad smell

stir
to mix soft or liquid things by moving them round with a spoon

stirrups
a rider's footrests hanging from each side of a horse's saddle

stitch
to sew with needle and thread

stocking
a long, close-fitting cover for your leg and foot

stomach
the part of the body where the food goes after being eaten

stone
1 a small piece of rock
2 the hard seed of some fruits like plums
3 a jewel

stool
a small seat without a back or arms

stoop
to bend forwards and downwards

stop
1 to end what you are doing
2 to come to a halt

store
1 a shop
2 to save things to use in the future

storey
a floor of a building with all its rooms

stork
a bird with a long beak and long legs

storm
bad weather with heavy rain or snow, strong winds and sometimes thunder

story
a tale that is true or made-up

stove
a cooker for food

awberry

stream

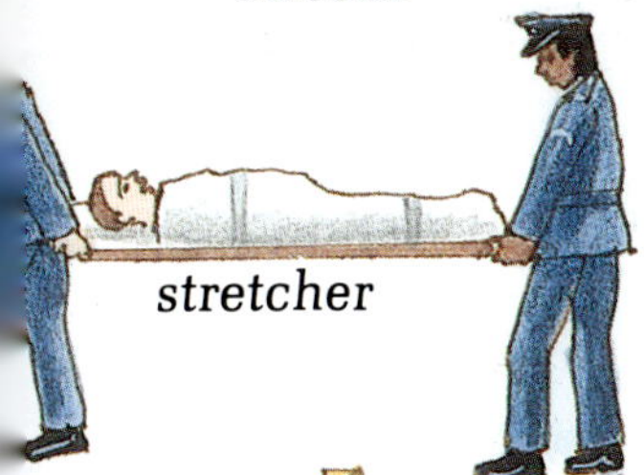

stretcher

io 1

studio 2

stowaway	someone who hides in a plane or ship to travel free
straight	*1* not bent or curved *2* honest; reliable
strange	*1* unusual; not common *2* not known, seen, or heard before
strap	a long, thin piece of leather
straw	*1* the dried stems of corn and other cereals *2* a thin tube used for sucking up a liquid
strawberry	the juicy red fruit of a plant that grows close to the ground
stray	*1* a lost child or animal *2* to wander about and get lost
stream	a small river
street	a road with buildings along its sides
strength	being strong; power
stretch	to make something longer by pulling it
stretcher	a frame of poles and material for carrying a sick or injured person
stride	a long pace or step
strike	*1* to hit something hard *2* to refuse to work because of some complaint *3* to light a match by rubbing it against something
string	thin cord
strip	*1* to undress; to uncover *2* a long, narrow piece of anything
stripe	a long, narrow mark or line
stroke	*1* to pass the hand gently over something *2* a mark made by a brush, crayon or pen
strong	powerful; having strength
struggle	to make a great effort
studio	*1* a place where an artist or a photographer works *2* a place where films are made, or where video or television programmes are produced
study	*1* to spend time learning *2* a room for quiet work
stuff	*1* material that a thing is made of *2* to pack full
stuffy	short of fresh air
stumble	to trip over and nearly fall
stupid	silly; foolish
sturdy	healthy; strong

submarine

subway 1

subway 2

sunflower

surfboard

sty
1 a place where pigs are kept
2 a painful swelling on the eyelid

submarine a ship that can travel under water

subtract to take away one thing from another

suburb an area of houses outside or near a town or city

subway
1 an underground passage built under a busy road
2 an electric, underground railway

succeed to manage to do what you are trying to do

suck to draw something into the mouth

sudden quick; not expected

suffer to feel pain

sufficient enough

sugar a sweet substance made from sugar cane or beet

suggest to offer an idea to other people

suit
1 a set of clothes to be worn together
2 to be right for
(Does this colour of dress **suit** you?)

suitcase a flat bag for carrying clothes

sultana a dried grape

sum
1 something to be worked out with figures
2 to add numbers and find the total
3 a certain amount of money

summer the season after spring; the warmest season

summit the top; the highest point

sun the body in the sky that gives the earth light and heat

sunflower a large, yellow flower that grows on a tall plant

sunrise the time when the sun comes up

sunset the time when the sun goes down

sunshine the light from the sun

supermarket a large store that sells foods and household goods

supersonic travelling faster than sound

supper the last meal of the day

sure certain

surf waves breaking on the seashore

surface the outside or top part

surfboard a shaped board for riding the waves as they break on the shore

surgeon a doctor who carries out operations on people

surgery where doctors, dentists and vets work

surprise something unexpected

surrender to give in

swallow
1 to pass food and drink down your throat
2 a small, dark blue and white bird with a forked tail

swamp an area of soft, very wet ground

swan a very large water-bird, usually white, that has a long neck

swarm a large number of insects moving together

sway to swing from side to side

swear
1 to make a promise
2 to use bad language

sweat the moisture from your skin when you are hot

sweater a thick, knitted jumper

sweep to clean something with a brush

sweet
1 tasting like sugar
2 a piece of toffee, chocolate etc
3 the pudding served at the end of a meal

swell to become bigger

swerve to change direction quickly

swift
1 fast; speedy; quick
2 a bird similar to a swallow

swim to move through the water using your arms and legs

swing
1 a seat hanging on ropes or chains on which you can push yourself
2 to move back and forth

switch
1 an instrument for turning things on and off
2 to change from one thing to another

swoop to move down quickly

sword a long steel blade with a handle

sycamore a large tree

synagogue a building where Jews worship

syrup a thick, sweet liquid

Tt

table a piece of furniture with a flat top and legs

tablet a small, flat piece of medicine

table tennis a game played on a table with bats and a very light ball

tadpole

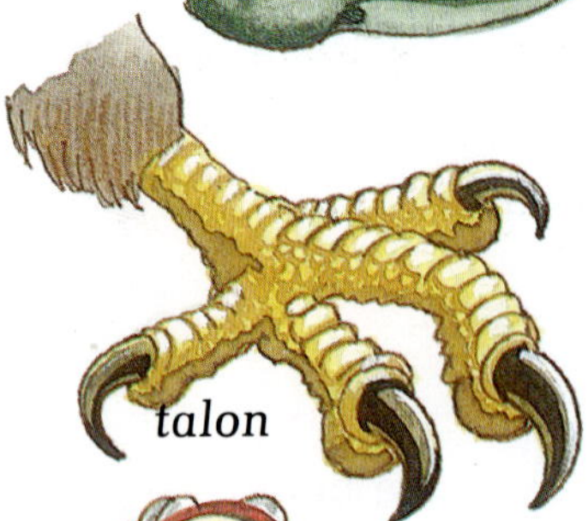
talon

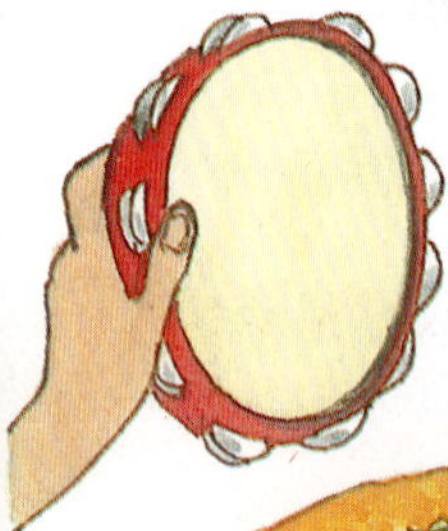
tambourine

tangerine

tarantula

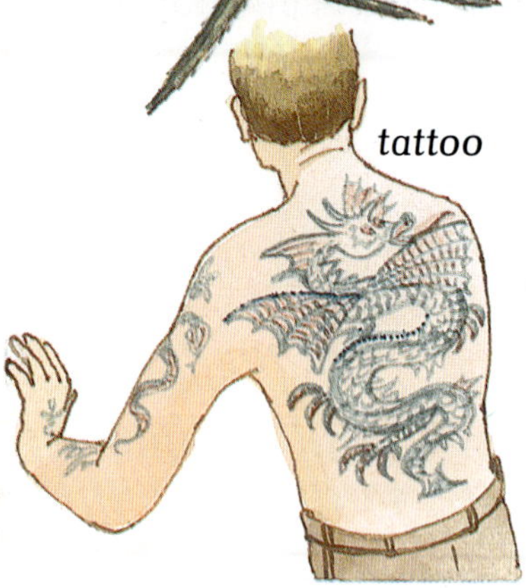
tattoo

tack
1 a small nail
2 to sail a zig-zag course against the wind

tackle the things you need for some kinds of sports or jobs

tadpole a young frog or toad just hatched out of its egg

tag a label

tail the part of an animal that sticks out at the back

tailor a person who makes clothes

take to get hold of and carry

take-off when an aircraft or rocket leaves the ground

tale a story

talk to speak; to say something

tall very high

talon the claw of a bird of prey such as an eagle, owl etc

tambourine a small, hand drum, with metal discs round the edge

tame not wild; friendly

tan
1 a light brown colour
2 become brown by being in the sun

tandem a two-seater bicycle

tangerine a small, sweet fruit like an orange

tank
1 a large container that holds liquid or gas
2 an armoured vehicle that moves on tracks

tanker a ship or lorry used to carry oil or other liquids

tap
1 to knock lightly
2 a handle which is turned to allow liquids or gas to flow

tape
1 a long, narrow strip of cloth
2 to record on a reel or cassette of plastic film

tape-recorder a machine that records sounds on a special tape, which can be played back later

tar a thick, black, sticky substance used in road-making

tarantula a large, hairy spider

target something to aim at

tart a small pie having fruit, custard or some other filling

tartan a woollen cloth having a pattern of stripes and squares, often used in Scotland for making kilts

task a job to be done

taste the flavour of food you eat

tattoo a coloured picture put on the skin

tax money paid by the people to pay for the things needed by the country

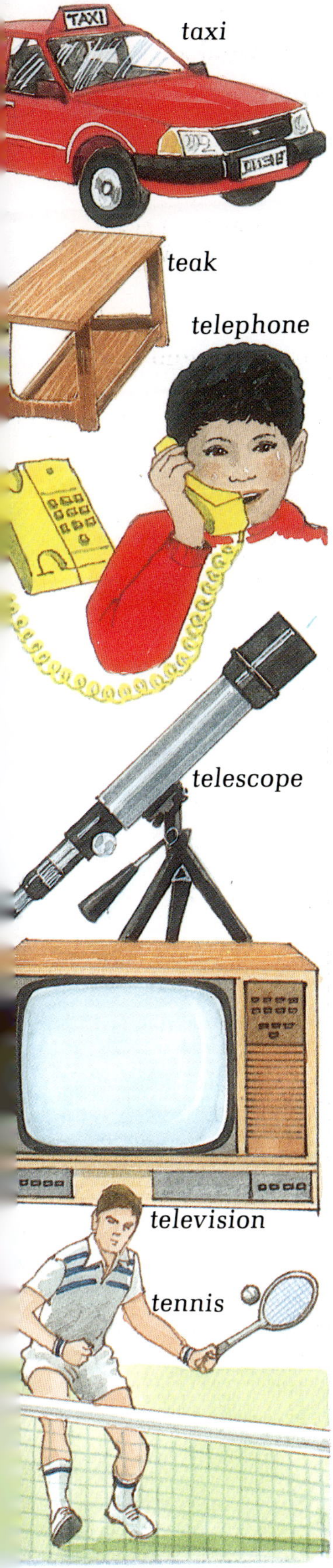

taxi a car you pay to ride in

tea 1 a drink made by pouring boiling water over dried leaves
2 a meal eaten at the end of the afternoon

teach to show people how to do things; to give lessons

teacher someone who teaches, usually in a school

teak a heavy, hard wood used in furniture making

team a group of people playing or working together

teapot a special jug for making tea

tear (like ear) a drop of water coming from your eye

tear (like bear) to pull apart; to rip

tease to make fun of somebody; to bother

teenager a person aged from 13 to 19

teeth more than one tooth

telephone an instrument enabling you to speak to people in another place

telescope an instrument with special lenses which make objects look larger and nearer

television an instrument that receives pictures and sound

tell to say; to give news by talking

temper the mood someone is in

temperature how hot or cold something is

temple 1 a building for prayer and worship
2 the part of the head between your forehead and ear

tempt to try to persuade someone to do something that is usually foolish or wrong

tender 1 soft; not tough
2 gentle and loving

tennis a game played by two or four people with rackets and a ball

tent a waterproof shelter placed over poles and held by ropes

tentacle a leg or feeler of some animals

term a period of time; a part of the school year

termite a small, ant-like insect that eats wood

terrace a row of houses joined together

terrible very bad; frightening

terrier a breed of dog

terrify to frighten very much

terror great fear; panic

theatre

thermometer

thimble

thorn

thrush

test
1 to find out how much someone knows
2 to try out

thank to say you are pleased and grateful

thaw the melting of snow and ice in mild weather

theatre a building where plays are acted

theft the act of stealing

their belonging to them; **their** clothes

then
1 at that time
2 for that reason
(If you have enough money, **then** you can go to the cinema.)

there in that place

thermometer an instrument that measures temperatures in degrees

thick
1 wide; not thin; a **thick** piece of bread
2 not watery; **thick** soup
3 hard to see through; **thick** fog

thief someone who steals

thimble a hard cover for the finger when using a needle

thin not fat; not thick; narrow

think to use your mind

thirsty wanting a drink

thistle a wild, prickly plant

thorn a sharp point on the stem of a plant

though even if

thought what is in your mind when thinking

thread
1 a thin string of cotton, silk, or other material used in sewing
2 to put thread through the eye of a needle

thrill an excited feeling

throat the inside of the neck, used for swallowing food and breathing

through from one end to the other; from one side to the other

throw to send something from the hand into the air

thrush a songbird with a brown and white speckled chest

thumb the short, thick finger on your hand

thump
1 a dull, heavy sound
2 a heavy blow

thunder the crash of noise following lightning, in a storm

tiara a woman's jewelled headband

tiger

tightrope

mber

tinsel

toadstool

tick
1 the sound made by a clock
2 a mark (✓) to show that something has been checked

ticket a card or paper to show that you have paid to travel by train, bus or plane, or to see a show

tickle to touch lightly to make someone giggle and laugh

tide the twice daily rise and fall of the sea

tidy neat; carefully arranged

tie
1 a narrow piece of cloth worn round the neck
2 to fasten with string or rope
3 to draw or be even in a game

tiger a fierce, striped animal of the cat family, living in parts of India and Asia

tight fitting very closely

tightrope a rope, high above the ground, that acrobats walk on

tights very close fitting stockings that cover the legs and body up to the waist

tile a piece of baked clay for covering a wall or a roof

till
1 up to; until
2 a drawer where money is kept in a shop

timber wood for building and making furniture

time
1 the hour shown on a clock
2 a measured period that something lasts

timid easily frightened; shy

tin
1 a silvery metal
2 a metal container; a can

tingle to have a prickly feeling

tinkle to make a light, ringing sound

tinsel glittering strips of material used for decoration

tiny very small

tip
1 a pointed end
2 to give money for a service done
3 to upset something
4 a piece of helpful advice or information

tiptoe to walk quietly on the tip of your toes

tired needing rest

tissue very thin, soft paper for wiping

toad an animal like a frog, but has rougher skin

toadstool a poisonous plant like a mushroom

toast bread that is made crisp and brown by heating it

tobacco the dried leaves of a plant used for smoking

tomahawk

tomato

torpedo

tortoise

toboggan a long sledge

today this day

toddler a small child just learning to walk

toe one of the five end parts of your foot

toffee a hard, sticky sweet

together with each other

toilet a bowl containing water, used for flushing away body waste

tomahawk a small axe, once used by North American Indians

tomato a soft fruit with a red skin

tomorrow the day after today

tongue the soft part inside your mouth that moves

tonight this night

tonne a measure of weight: 1000 kilograms

tonsils the small, oval pieces of flesh in the back of the throat

too
1 also; as well
(I am going for a walk, and Sarah is coming **too**.)
2 more than enough
(You have eaten **too** many sweets!)

tool something to help you to do work

tooth one of the bonelike parts of the mouth, used for chewing and biting

toothache a pain in a tooth

toothbrush a brush for cleaning teeth

toothpaste a very thick liquid used to clean your teeth

top
1 the highest point
2 a toy which can be made to spin

torch an electric light that you can carry

tornado a very strong, whirling wind that destroys whatever it touches

torpedo a rocket-shaped shell fired through the water usually against ships

tortoise a slow-moving animal covered by a shell

torture to cause horrible pain

toss to throw up into the air

total everything added together

totem pole a carved or painted pole made by North American Indians

touch
1 to feel with your fingers or some other part of your body
2 to be against

tough
1 not easily broken or bent
2 hard to chew

tourist a person on holiday who travels about to see different places

tow to drag; to pull something using a rope or chain

towards in the direction of

towel a piece of cloth for drying things

tower a tall, narrow building

town a large number of houses, shops, offices and other buildings

toy something to play with

track
1 a narrow path
2 a railway line
3 a racecourse
4 marks on the ground left by something moving

tractor a powerful vehicle for pulling farm machinery and heavy loads

trade
1 the buying and selling of things
2 the work that we do

traffic the movement of vehicles and people

traffic-lights coloured lights to control traffic

traffic-warden a person who controls traffic and parking

trail
1 to follow a track or the scent
2 to follow behind

trailer a vehicle pulled by another vehicle

train
1 railway coaches or wagons joined to an engine
2 to practise for something

traitor someone who is disloyal to his or her friends, or country

tram an electric passenger car that runs on rails

tramp
1 a poor person who has no home, and wanders from place to place
2 to walk with heavy steps

trampoline a piece of canvas held to a frame by strong springs on which people jump up and down

transfer to move things or people from one place to another

translate to put into another language

transparent clear; able to be seen through

transport to move goods or people from place to place

trap
1 a way to catch animals
2 a plan for catching someone

trapeze		a swinging bar held by two ropes, used by acrobats
travel		to move about from place to place
trawler		a fishing boat which catches fish by dragging a large net
tray		a flat board for carrying things
treacle		a dark, sticky liquid made from sugar
treasure		something very valuable
treat	*1*	to make a gift
	2	to behave in a certain way towards someone
tree		a large plant with a trunk, branches and leaves
tremble		to shiver or shake
trench		a narrow ditch dug in the ground
triangle		a shape with three sides
trick	*1*	something done to play a joke on or to surprise
	2	to cheat other people
tricycle		a cycle having three wheels
trio		a group of three singers or musicians
trip	*1*	to stumble and fall
	2	a journey
trolley	*1*	a small table on wheels
	2	a small handcart
trombone		a musical instrument that you play by blowing into it and sliding a tube
tropics		the hot parts of the world either side of the equator
trot		to run gently with small steps
trouble		anything that bothers or disturbs you
trousers		a garment with two legs
trout		a freshwater fish
trowel	*1*	a small, garden tool
	2	a tool for spreading cement, plaster etc
truck		a motor vehicle for carrying heavy loads
true		correct; honest
trumpet		a metal wind instrument
trunk	*1*	the main part of a tree
	2	an elephant's long nose
	3	a large box for carrying clothes etc
try	*1*	to attempt
	2	a score in rugby
	3	to test something
T-shirt		a close-fitting shirt without sleeves

tuna

tulip

tub a large container for holding a liquid

tube
1 a pipe made of metal, glass, rubber or plastic
2 the London underground railway

tug
1 a sharp pull
2 a small, powerful boat used for towing and pushing large ships in and out of a harbour

tulip a colourful flower that grows from a bulb

tumble to fall down

tumbler a drinking glass

tuna a large sea-fish

tundra a large area of flat, treeless land in the Arctic

tune a number of pleasing musical notes

tunnel an underground passage

turban a head-dress made up from a piece of cloth

turkey a large bird raised for food

tundra

turn
1 to face a different way
2 to move round like a wheel
3 a chance to do something

turnip a plant with a large, round root used as a vegetable

turquoise a greenish-blue colour

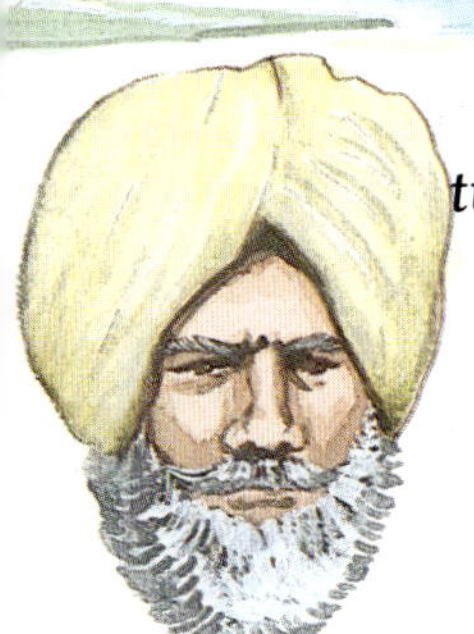

turban

turtle an animal that lives on land or in the sea; it has a hard shell and moves slowly

tusk a long, pointed tooth or bone found in certain animals such as the elephant and walrus

twice two times

twig a small branch of a tree or bush

twilight the dim light between sunset and darkness

turkey

twin one of two children born at the same time

twinkle to sparkle

twist to turn round something

type
1 a kind
2 printed letters
3 to print words by using a typewriter

typhoon a very bad storm with rain and strong wind

tyre the rubber round the outside of a wheel

turtle

Uu

ugly not pretty or nice to look at

ukelele a musical instrument with four strings

umpire

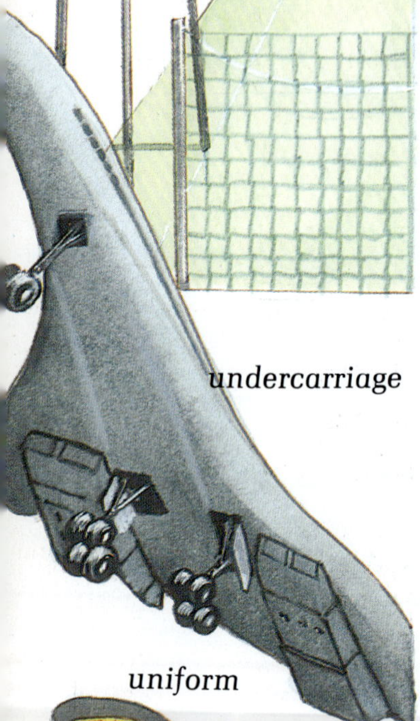

undercarriage

uniform

umbrella a covered frame to keep off the rain

umpire a person who sees that the rules of a game are followed

unable not able

uncle a brother of your father or mother; an aunt's husband

under below; beneath

undercarriage the wheels and axles of an aeroplane

undergrowth small plants and bushes growing close to the ground

understand to know what something means

underwear clothes you wear under your outer clothes

undo to unfasten

undress to take off your clothes

unemployed out of work

unequal not the same in size or amount

uneven not even or level

unhappy not happy; sad

uniform special clothes worn to show that people belong to the same group such as policemen, soldiers, scouts etc

unite to join together

universe everything that exists on the earth and in space

university a place of learning for older students

unkind not kind; cruel

unless if not
(You will not pass your driving test **unless** you practise more.)

unload to take off a load

unlucky having bad luck or out of luck

untidy not tidy; not neat

untie to undo something that has been tied

until up to the time when

unusual not usual; strange

unwell not well; ill

up from a lower to a higher place

uproar a very loud shouting; a noisy disturbance

upset
1 to knock down or over
2 to make unhappy

upstairs on a higher floor of a building

urgent needing to be done at once

vacuum cleaner

cuum flask

use	to do something with
useful	of some use
useless	of no use
usual	often done; normal
utensil	a piece of equipment, usually one used in the kitchen

Vv

valentine

vacant	empty
vacation	a holiday
vacuum cleaner	a machine that cleans carpets, floors etc, by suction
vacuum flask	a container for keeping drinks hot or cold
vague	not clear; uncertain
vain	proud; conceited
valentine	a card sent on St Valentine's Day, February 14th
valley	low ground between two hills or mountains
valuable	having great value; worth much money
value	the importance or worth of something
van	a covered vehicle for carrying goods
vandal	someone who destroys property
vanilla	flavouring used in ice-cream, blancmange etc
vanish	to go out of sight
vapour	steam from boiling water; mist
various	different from one another
vase	a container for holding flowers
vault	a safe room that is used to store money, jewels, or other things of value
veal	the meat of a calf
vegetable	a plant grown for food
vehicle	something which moves, such as a car, van, lorry, bus etc
veil	a thin cloth covering for the face
vein	one of the thin tubes that carries blood in the body to the heart
velvet	a smooth, soft, thick cloth
venison	the meat from a deer
venom	the poison of some snakes and spiders

ult

veil

Uu Vv

veranda

viaduct

violet

violin

volcano

ventriloquist		an entertainer who seems to be able to make a puppet speak
veranda		an outdoor platform with a roof, joined to a house
verge		the edge; the border
vermin		harmful creatures such as rats, mice etc
vertical		straight up and down
vessel	*1*	a ship or large boat
	2	a container for liquids
vest		an undergarment worn next to the skin
vet		an animal doctor; a veterinary surgeon
vex		to annoy
viaduct		a long bridge with many arches
vibrate		to tremble; to shake
vicar		a clergyman; a Christian priest
victory		win in a game, contest or battle
video recorder		a machine used for recording television pictures and sound on a special tape
view		everything that you can see from one place
village		a small group of houses in the country
vine		a plant on which grapes grow
vinegar		a sour liquid used for flavouring and preserving food
violet		a tiny flower with blue, purple, or white flowers
violin		a musical instrument that has four strings and is played with a bow
visible		able to be seen
visit		to call to see someone
vitamin		a substance needed for good health, found in sunshine and many foods
vocabulary	*1*	all the words you know and use
	2	a list of words
voice		the sound from your mouth when you are speaking or singing
volcano		a mountain which can throw out liquid rock, hot ashes, steam and flames
volume	*1*	the amount of space something fills
	2	a book
vomit		to be sick
vowel		any of the five letters a, e, i, o, u
voyage		a journey by sea, or through space

vulture

wagon

'laby

walnut

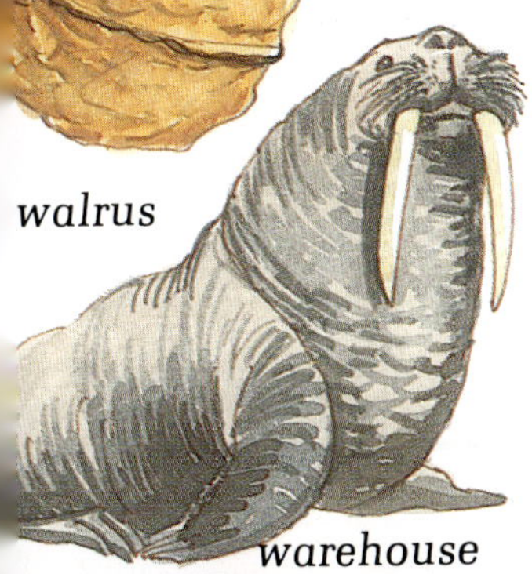

walrus

warehouse

vulture	a large bird that feeds on dead animals

Ww

waddle	to walk like a duck
wade	to walk through shallow water
wafer	a thin biscuit, often eaten with ice-cream
wag	to move quickly from side to side
wage	money paid for work done
wagon	a vehicle used for carrying heavy loads, such as a railway truck
wail	a long, sad cry
waist	the part of your body between the ribs and hips
waistcoat	a short jacket without sleeves
wait	to stay in one place until something happens or someone comes
waiter/waitress	someone who serves food to people in a restaurant
wake	to rouse from sleep
walk	to move on the feet
wall	a side of a building or a room
wallaby	a small kind of kangaroo
wallet	a flat, folding case for holding money, cards and photographs etc
wallpaper	a paper, often with a pattern, that is used to decorate the walls of a room
walnut	a hard, round nut with a crinkled shell
walrus	a large sea animal, something like a seal, that has two tusks
wander	to move about from one place to another, not sure of where you want to go
want	to wish to have
war	a fight between countries
ward	a room for patients in a hospital
warder	someone who looks after prisoners
wardrobe	a cupboard for clothes
warehouse	a large building where goods are stored
warm	fairly hot
warn	to tell someone about possible danger or trouble
wart	a small, hard lump on the skin

washer 1

washer 2

wasp

water-ski

weasel

wash		to clean with soap and water
washer	1	a machine for washing
	2	a flat ring, usually of metal or rubber
wasp		a stinging insect
waste	1	rubbish; useless things
	2	to use without care
watch	1	to look at carefully
	2	a small clock usually worn on the wrist
	3	to be on guard
water		the liquid that falls as rain and found in rivers, lakes and the sea
waterfall		a stream of water falling from a high place
waterproof		any material through which water cannot go
water-ski		to glide over water on water skis while being pulled by a towing rope attached to a speed-boat
wave	1	a rippling movement of water
	2	to move the hand from side to side
wax	1	a substance made by bees
	2	the material used to make candles and polish
way	1	how to do something
	2	a road; a path; a direction
weak		not strong
wealthy		having a lot of money or property
weapon		anything used for fighting or hunting
wear	1	to be dressed in something
	2	to become damaged or weak by much use
weary		tired
weasel		a small, thin wild animal that lives on smaller animals such as mice and birds
weather		how wet or dry, or hot or cold the air is outside
weave		to make cloth from threads
web		a net of sticky threads spun by a spider
wedding		the time when a man and woman become husband and wife
weed		any wild plant growing in places where it is not wanted
week		a period of seven days
weekend		from Friday night until Sunday evening
weep		to cry; to sob
weigh		to find the mass or heaviness of something
weird		very strange

welcome		to greet someone in a friendly way
well	*1*	in good health
	2	a deep hole in the ground with water or oil at the bottom
	3	in a good way (You played **well.**)
wellingtons		long rubber boots
west		the direction of sunset; the opposite to east
wet		full of liquid or covered with a liquid
whale		a huge sea animal that has a body like a fish but is a mammal
wharf		a loading and unloading place for ships
wheat		a grain made into flour
wheel		a ring of wood, plastic, or metal that can turn round on an axle
wheelbarrow		a handcart with one wheel used by gardeners and builders
wheelchair		a chair on wheels for the use of people who can't walk
whimper		to cry softly
whine		a long, sad sound
whinny		a cry made by a horse
whip	*1*	a piece of thin leather or cord on a handle
	2	to stir a liquid so that it has a foam
whirl		to spin round quickly
whirlwind		a very strong wind that blows round and round
whiskers		hair growing on the face
whisky		a very strong drink made from grain
whisper		to speak very softly
whistle	*1*	a high sharp sound
	2	an instrument for making a whistling sound
white		the colour of fresh snow
whole		complete; with nothing missing
wick		a string in a candle or oil lamp
wicked		very bad; evil
wicket		the three stumps and bails in cricket
wide		measuring a long way from one side to other
widow		a woman whose husband is dead
widower		a man whose wife is dead
width		how wide something is
wife		a married woman

wigwam

willow

windmill

wolf

woodpecker

wig		false hair to cover the head
wigwam		a hut that some North American Indians used to live in
wild	*1*	living freely; not tame
	2	very windy; stormy
wildebeest		a South African antelope often called a gnu
wilderness		an open stretch of country where no one lives
willing		glad and ready to do something
willow		a tree with long, narrow leaves, and thin branches
win		to beat others in a game or contest
wind (say find)		to twist around or wrap around
wind (say pinned)		quickly moving air
windmill		a tower with sails that turn in the wind
window		an opening in the wall of a building to let in light
wine		a strong drink made from grapes or other fruit
wing	*1*	one of the parts of a bird, bat or insect used for flying
	2	a part of an aeroplane
wink		to close and open an eyelid quickly
winter		the coldest season of the year
wipe		to dry or clean with a cloth
wire		a metal thread
wise		having plenty of sense
wish		to desire something
witch		a woman in fairy tales who is thought to have magic powers
wizard		a man in fairy tales who is thought to have magic powers
wobble		to stagger; to sway from side to side
wolf		a wild animal, usually grey, that looks like a dog
woman		a grown-up female person
wonder	*1*	a feeling of surprise; amazement
	2	to want to know
wood	*1*	a number of trees growing together
	2	the hard part of a tree, under the bark
woodpecker		a bird that has a strong, pointed bill
wool		the thick hair from sheep and lambs
work		something that you have to do to earn a living
world		the earth and everything on it
worm		a small, thin animal with a soft body and no legs that lives in soil or sand

wren

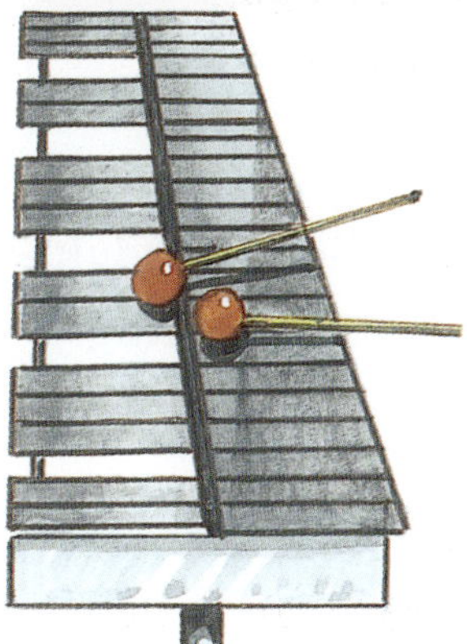
xylophone

yak

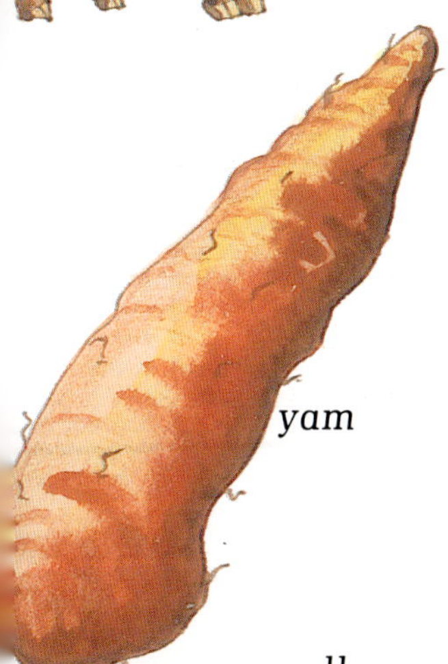
yam

yellow

worry to feel troubled; to be uneasy

wound an injury such as a cut

wrap to cover something all round

wreck
1 anything destroyed, such as a ship on rocks or a crashed aircraft
2 to destroy; to ruin

wren a tiny, brown, songbird

wrestle to struggle with a person

wriggle to twist and turn

wrinkle a line or crease in cloth or on the skin

wrist the joint between your hand and arm

write to put down letters or words on paper

wrong
1 not correct
2 not fair; bad
(It is **wrong** to steal.)

Xx

X-rays special rays that are used to take a picture of the inside of your body

xylophone a musical instrument played by hitting bars with a wooden hammer

Yy

yacht a sailing boat

yak a type of ox

yam a kind of sweet potato

yard
1 a measure of length equal to a little less than one metre
2 an enclosed space

yarn
1 a thick thread used in sewing, weaving, or knitting
2 a story

yawn to open your mouth wide and breathe in deeply when tired or bored

year a measure of time; twelve months; 365 days

yeast a substance used to make dough rise when making bread

yell to shout very loudly

yellow a colour; the colour of a dandelion

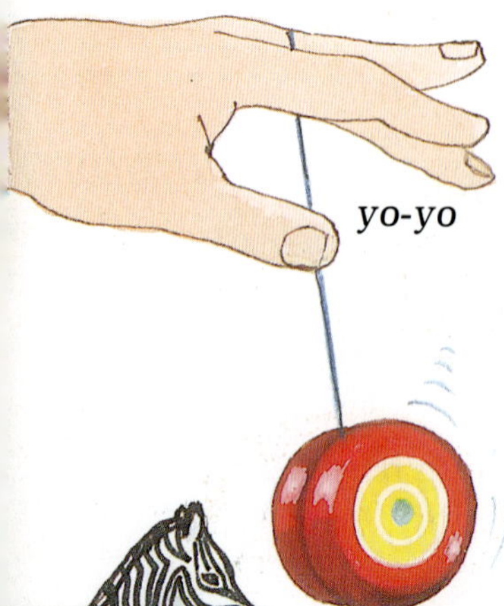

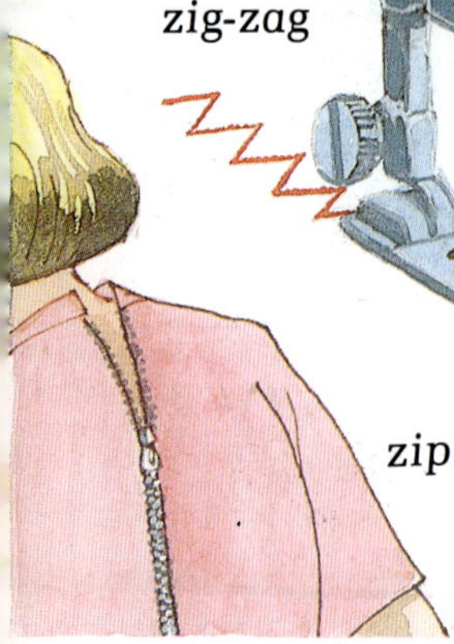

yesterday	the day before today
yet	up to now
yew	an evergreen tree with red berries
yogurt	a thick, creamy food made from milk
yolk	the yellow part of an egg
young	not old; not grown up
your	belonging to you
youth	the time between being a child and being an adult
yo-yo	a small toy that is spun up and down on a string

Zz

zebra	a wild animal like a horse with black and white stripes
zebra-crossing	a specially marked part of a road where people can cross safely
zero	nought; the figure 0
zigzag	a line with many sharp turns
zinc	a greyish-white metal
zip	a sliding fastener used on clothes
zoo	a place where wild animals are kept for people to look at them

Numbers

Numbers that are used a lot

1	one	first
2	two	second
3	three	third
4	four	fourth
5	five	fifth
6	six	sixth
7	seven	seventh
8	eight	eighth
9	nine	ninth
10	ten	tenth
11	eleven	eleventh
12	twelve	twelfth
13	thirteen	thirteenth
14	fourteen	fourteenth
15	fifteen	fifteenth
16	sixteen	sixteenth
17	seventeen	seventeenth
18	eighteen	eighteenth
19	nineteen	nineteenth
20	twenty	twentieth
21	twenty-one	twenty-first
30	thirty	thirtieth
40	forty	fortieth
50	fifty	fiftieth
60	sixty	sixtieth
70	seventy	seventieth
80	eighty	eightieth
90	ninety	ninetieth
100	one hundred	hundredth
1000	one thousand	thousandth
1 000 000	one million	millionth
1 000 000 000	one billion	billionth

Measures (SI units)

Length

10 millimetres (mm)	=	1 centimetre (cm)
100 centimetres	=	1 metre (m)
1000 metres	=	1 Kilometre (Km)
1 metre	=	39.37 inches (in)

Mass and Weight

10 milligrams (mg)	=	1 centigram (cg)
100 centigrams	=	1 gram (g)
1000 grams	=	1 Kilogram (Kg)
1000 Kilograms	=	1 tonne

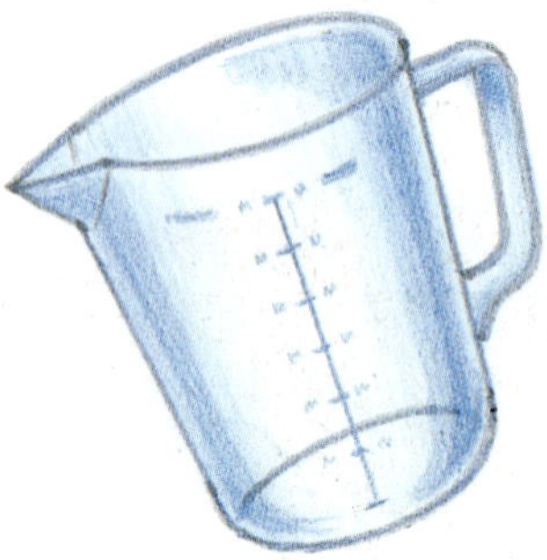

Capacity

10 millilitres (ml)	=	1 centilitre (cl)
100 centilitres	=	1 Litre (l)
1000 litres	=	1 Kilolitre (Kl)
1000 millilitres	=	1 litre

Mathematical Signs

+ plus	− minus
× multiplied by	÷ divided by
= is equal to	≠ is not equal to
< greater than	> less than
° degree	% percentage

Flat Shapes

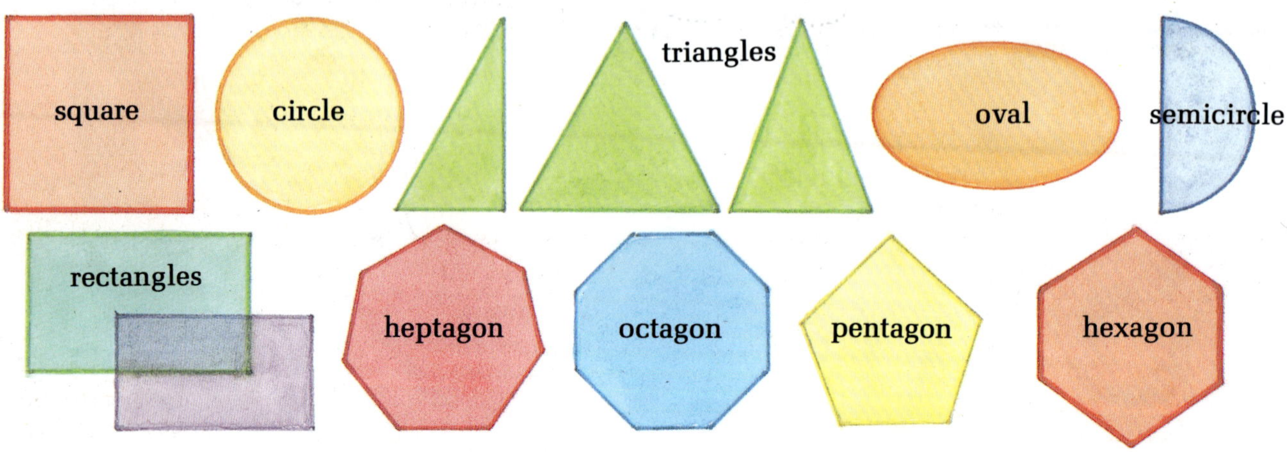

Solid Shapes

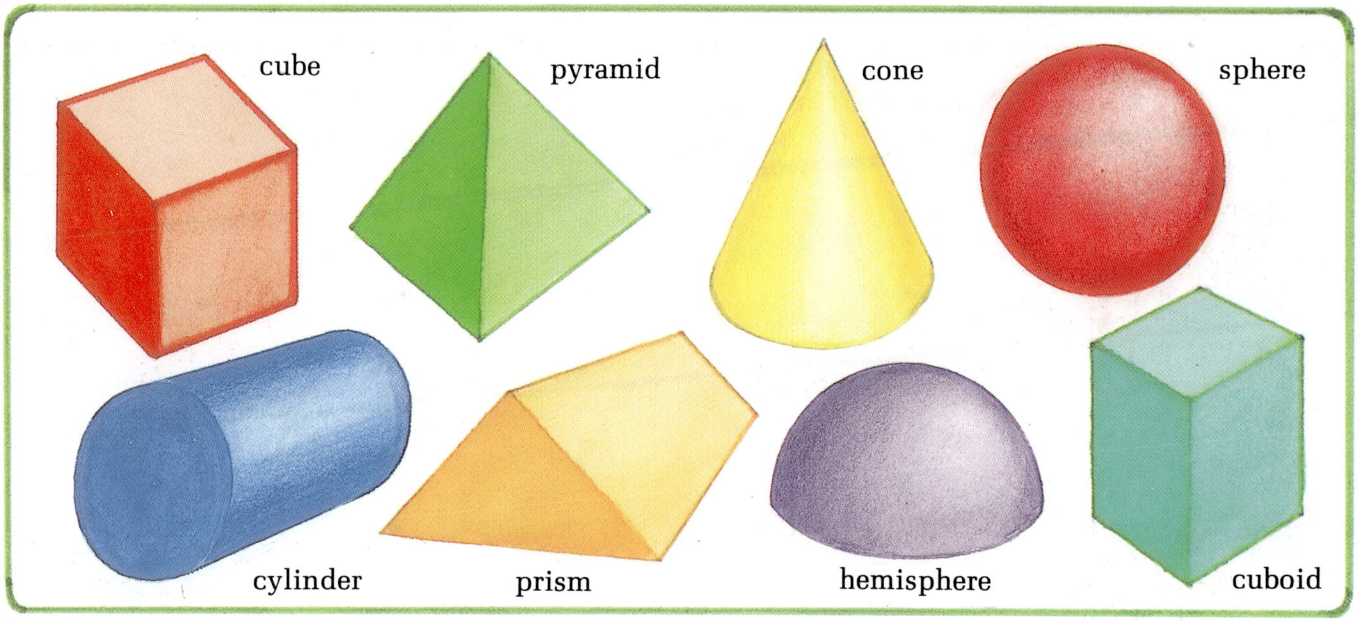

Time

60 seconds	=	1 minute
60 minutes	=	1 hour
24 hours	=	1 day
7 days	=	1 week
365 days, 52 weeks, 12 months	=	1 year
366 days	=	1 leap year
10 years	=	a decade
100 years	=	a century

Days

Sunday	(Sun.)	Monday	(Mon.)	Tuesday	(Tues.)
Wednesday	(Wed.)	Thursday	(Thurs.)	Friday	(Frid.)
Saturday	(Sat.)				

Months

January	(Jan.)	31days	July	(July)	31 days
February	(Feb.)	28	August	(Aug.)	31
March	(Mar.)	31	September	(Sept.)	30
April	(Apr.)	30	October	(Oct.)	31
May	(May)	31	November	(Nov.)	30
June	(June)	30	December	(Dec.)	31

Continents

Africa Antarctica Asia Australia Europe North America South America

Planets Mercury Venus Earth Mars Jupiter Saturn Uranus Neptune Pluto